Persistence Best Practices f[...] Applications

Effective strategies for distributed cloud-native applications and data-driven modernization

Otávio Santana

Karina Varela

‹packt›

BIRMINGHAM—MUMBAI

Persistence Best Practices for Java Applications

Copyright © 2023 Packt Publishing

All rights reserved. No part of this book may be reproduced, stored in a retrieval system, or transmitted in any form or by any means, without the prior written permission of the publisher, except in the case of brief quotations embedded in critical articles or reviews.

Every effort has been made in the preparation of this book to ensure the accuracy of the information presented. However, the information contained in this book is sold without warranty, either express or implied. Neither the author(s), nor Packt Publishing or its dealers and distributors, will be held liable for any damages caused or alleged to have been caused directly or indirectly by this book.

Packt Publishing has endeavored to provide trademark information about all of the companies and products mentioned in this book by the appropriate use of capitals. However, Packt Publishing cannot guarantee the accuracy of this information.

Group Product Manager: Gebin George

Publishing Product Manager: Kunal Sawant

Senior Editor: Nisha Cleetus

Technical Editor: Shruti Thingalaya

Copy Editor: Safis Editing

Project Coordinator: Deeksha Thakkar

Proofreader: Safis Editing

Indexer: Pratik Shirodkar

Production Designer: Shankar Kalbhor

Business Development Executive: Kriti Sharma

Developer Relations Marketing Executives: Rayyan Khan and Sonia Chauhan

First published: August 2023

Production reference: 2040823

Published by Packt Publishing Ltd.
Grosvenor House
11 St Paul's Square
Birmingham
B3 1RB, UK.

ISBN 978-1-83763-127-8

www.packtpub.com

To my wife, Poliana, my loving partner, and God's blessing throughout our journey.

– Otávio Santana

To Ian, my endless inspiration. Your belief in me, patient support, and encouragement mean the world. May this book ignite your passion and dedication. I'm proud to call you my son.

– Karina Varela

Contributors

About the authors

Otávio Santana is a passionate architect and software engineer with expertise in the cloud, Java, and polyglot persistence. He contributes to open source projects, leads Java specifications, and works on NoSQL databases. He represents SouJava in the Java Community Process and Jakarta EE boards, mentors developers, and writes articles and books on software architecture. As a global speaker, he presents at major conferences and supports Java User Groups. Otávio has received numerous awards and is a member of Java Champions and Oracle ACE. He enjoys history, traveling, and telling dad jokes in multiple languages.

Karina Varela is a highly experienced cloud solutions expert with a strong background in Java and open source culture. Having worked at Red Hat and IBM, she brings valuable expertise in developing, delivering, and troubleshooting production applications. Karina's contributions extend beyond technical skills, as she has played a crucial role in deploying mission-critical software globally. She is well regarded in the Java community for her insightful writings and speeches at tech conferences. Karina actively supports the open source community and leads widely used enterprise solutions. Her innovative approach and commitment to quality have made a significant impact on the industry, establishing her as a thought leader and influential contributor.

About the reviewer

Alain Trottier is a seasoned computer engineer with a passion for communicating technology and driving innovation. He has dedicated two decades to exploring the ever-evolving world of software engineering. Throughout his career, he has channeled his expertise into authoring magazine articles and publishing four comprehensive books on software engineering. Additionally, he has contributed as a technical editor for several notable publications in the field. Recognized as an intrapreneur, he has consistently sought opportunities to innovate and deliver value within organizations. He invites you to connect with him on LinkedIn (`https://www.linkedin.com/in/alaintrottier`) to explore the possibilities of collaboration, share insights, and engage in meaningful conversations about the exciting realm of technology and innovation. Let's make a difference together.

Table of Contents

Part 1: Persistence in Cloud Computing – Storing and Managing Data in Modern Software Architecture

1

2

3

Exploring Architectural Strategies and Cloud Usage   23

4

Design Patterns for Data Management in Cloud-Native Applications   39

Part 2: Jakarta EE, MicroProfile, Modern Persistence Technologies, and Their Trade-Offs

5

Jakarta EE and JPA – State of Affairs   61

6

7

8

Part 3: Architectural Perspective over Persistence

9

10

11

12

Preface

A solid software architecture combines every building block required to bring a tech solution to life. In the early days of an application's life, the design and practices are established: microservice or monolith architecture, event-driven approach, the integration and delivery application life cycle, containerization, and so on. Restricting the application side, especially in a Java context, frameworks and execution runtimes are also defined. Like the good old legacy systems, most modern cloud-native solutions rely on data, generally in data stores (e.g., databases). Unfortunately, the persistence layer is often left aside and not treated with the same importance as these other topics. For scenarios dependent on stateful services, this is the beginning of the end – the brand-new solution is doomed for a life of performance struggles and reduced maintainability, or even worse, might have ingrained weeds causing data inconsistency. The reduced maintainability is a result of the neglect in the persistence layer design and definitions, as schemes and data models are poorly implemented on top of insufficient information. In such scenarios, even trivial database refactorings are brutal and time-consuming.

Having a panoramic understanding of the challenges, solutions, and best practices of the persistence layer, technologies, and existing approaches is the way out of such troublesome scenarios and many more related to applications and data stores.

This book presents well-established patterns and standards that can be used in Java solutions, with valuable pros and cons of the trendy technologies and frameworks used in cloud-native microservices when confronted with good Java coding practices. As Java technologies have been broadly used for over two decades now, cloud adoption puts extra challenges on the table, such as the growing need for cost reduction through stack modernization. So, you will learn about application modernization strategies and gain in-depth knowledge about how enterprise data integration patterns and event-driven architectures enable smooth modernization processes with low-to-zero impact on the existing legacy stack.

After reading this book, your next architectural decision will be solid and backed by a thorough explanation of data storage options and their respective recommended usage scenarios, covering technologies such as SQL, NoSQL, and NewSQL. When talking about data-related content tailored within a Java ecosystem's context, extensive information is available on topics such as how MicroProfile and Jakarta EE work; database patterns (such as Active Record and **Data Access Object** (**DAO**); **Command and Query Responsibility Segregation** (**CQRS**); in-memory persistence; and frameworks for object mapping.

If, at this point, you understand the reasons why the careful handling of data storage is crucial for a system and architecture and believe it has a direct impact on the whole organization, to the point of adding such value that businesses strive to beat their competitors by adopting data-centric strategies, then this book is for you. Get ready to join us on this exciting journey of exploring data, its mysteries, and its treasures in a cloud-driven era.

Who this book is for

This book is primarily intended for experienced developers, engineers, and software architects with a strong background in Java and focused on building Java solutions. It is designed to cater to individuals who already possess a solid understanding of Java development and seek to enhance their knowledge and skills in persistence.

The content of this book assumes a certain level of familiarity with Java programming concepts, object-oriented design principles, and enterprise application development. It dives into advanced topics and explores various aspects of persistence in modern Java solutions.

Whether you are a seasoned Java developer looking to deepen your understanding of persistence technologies, an engineer seeking to optimize performance and scalability in Java applications, or a software architect responsible for designing robust persistence layers, this book provides valuable insights, best practices, and practical guidance to meet your needs.

By leveraging the expertise and experience shared in this book, you can enhance your ability to design, implement, and optimize persistence solutions within your Java projects, ultimately empowering you to develop high-performing, scalable, and maintainable Java applications.

What this book covers

Chapter 1, *Storing Data: from the Caves to the Clouds*, is where you will acquire the foundation knowledge you'll need for what's coming next in the book, so buckle up. You will learn about the challenges of storing data, which gave birth to the first data storage solutions. As technology advanced, databases evolved into robust and reliable solutions. The Java ecosystem responded well and grew along with the data ecosystem, providing users with frameworks, application servers, and so on to allow for a simpler developer experience yet deliver performant database integration.

Chapter 2, *Distilling the Multiple Database Flavors*, discusses how a polyglot persistence strategy naturally materializes with the growth and individual needs of decoupled and independent services. You will explore different ways to store data, market data management systems (e.g., relational, NoSQL, and NewSQL), their respective languages, and, most importantly, the use case scenarios for each of them. Overengineering is the villain in system design, so this chapter will prepare you with the knowledge to keep it far from your persistence layer.

Chapter 3, *Exploring Architectural Strategies and Cloud Usage*, will get you familiar with and help you recall concepts around the multiple ways to architect solutions. You will learn about the relationship between monoliths, microservices, and event-driven solutions, and how these approaches push the increasing adoption of different cloud service offerings. You will learn how to identify the benefits and disadvantages of using a mix of on-premises and cloud solutions, a mix that results in organizations' solutions being built on top of hybrid and/or multi-cloud models.

Chapter 4, Getting the Most out of Design Patterns for Data Management in Cloud-Native Applications, dives into the realm of data management in cloud-native applications and explores how to leverage design patterns effectively. With the increasing adoption of cloud technologies, it has become crucial for developers to optimize data management strategies to maximize the benefits of cloud-native architectures.

Chapter 5, Jakarta EE and JPA: State of Affairs, provides a comprehensive overview of persistence within the Jakarta EE and MicroProfile ecosystems. Persistence is a fundamental aspect of enterprise application development, and understanding how it is handled in these frameworks is essential for developers.

Chapter 6, NoSQL in Java Demystified: One API to Rule Them All, talks about how NoSQL databases open the doors to various capabilities in enterprise applications and systems. Nowadays, even more-conservative markets such as finance are starting to consider non-relational database solutions. It's time to get familiar with NoSQL databases and their types, how to integrate them with Java services, and the use cases where they may be a good fit for data storage.

Chapter 7, The Missing Guide for jOOQ Adoption, discusses object-oriented querying, commonly known as jOOQ, which is a light database-mapping software library in Java that implements the Active Record pattern. Its purpose is to be relational and object-oriented by providing a **domain-specific language (DSL)** to construct queries from classes automatically generated based on a database schema.

Chapter 8, Ultra-Fast In-Memory Persistence with Eclipse Store, explores Eclipse Store, which delivers ultra-fast in-memory data processing with pure Java. It provides microsecond query time, low-latency data access, gigantic data throughput, and workloads. Thus, it saves lots of CPU power, CO_2 emissions, and costs in the data center.

Chapter 9, Persistence Practices: Exploring Polyglot Persistence, delves into the concept of polyglot persistence within the Jakarta Data ecosystem. Polyglot persistence refers to the practice of using multiple data storage technologies within an application to optimize for different data requirements.

Chapter 10, Architecting Distributed Systems: Challenges and Anti-Patterns, explores the intricacies of architecting distributed systems and examines the challenges and anti-patterns that can arise in the process. Distributed systems are becoming increasingly prevalent in modern software architecture, but they come with their own set of complexities.

Chapter 11, Modernization Strategies and Data Integration, explores modernization strategies and data integration techniques to help organizations adapt their existing systems to meet the demands of modern technology landscapes. As technology evolves rapidly, it becomes crucial for businesses to modernize their legacy systems and integrate them seamlessly with new technologies.

Chapter 12, Final Considerations on Persistence in Modern Java Solutions, is the final chapter, and we provide important considerations and insights regarding persistence in modern Java solutions. As the landscape of Java development evolves, it is crucial to stay up to date with best practices and emerging trends in persistence.

To get the most out of this book

Before you begin reading this book and diving into the software requirements, it is crucial to understand the following technologies: Java 17, Maven, Git, and Docker. Familiarity with Java 17 is assumed, including knowledge of its syntax and object-oriented programming concepts and familiarity with core libraries and frameworks. Understanding Maven will be beneficial, as it is a popular build automation tool for managing dependencies and building Java projects. Proficiency in Git, a version control system, is necessary to track and manage source code changes effectively. Lastly, knowledge of Docker, a containerization platform, will help with understanding how to package and deploy software applications in isolated environments.

Software/hardware covered in the book	Operating system requirements
Java 17	Windows, macOS, or Linux
Maven	
Git	
Docker	

If you are using the digital version of this book, we advise you to type the code yourself or access the code from the book's GitHub repository (a link is available in the next section). Doing so will help you avoid any potential errors related to the copying and pasting of code.

Download the example code files

You can download the example code files for this book from GitHub at `https://github.com/PacktPublishing/Persistence-Best-Practices-for-Java-Applications/`. If there's an update to the code, it will be updated in the GitHub repository.

Conventions used

There are a number of text conventions used throughout this book.

`Code in text`: Indicates code words in text, database table names, folder names, filenames, file extensions, pathnames, dummy URLs, user input, and Twitter handles. Here is an example: "In this domain, the Book entity attributes should be `title`, `author`, `publisher`, and `genre`."

A block of code is set as follows:

```
public class Book {
    private final String title;
    private final String author;
    private final String publisher;
    private final String genre;
    // constructor method
    // builder inner class
}
```

When we wish to draw your attention to a particular part of a code block, the relevant lines or items are set in bold:

```
public class Book {
    private final String title;
    private final String author;
    private final String publisher;
    private final String genre;
    // constructor method
    // builder inner class
}
```

Any command-line input or output is written as follows:

```
$ mkdir css
$ cd css
```

Bold: Indicates a new term, an important word, or words that you see onscreen. For instance, words in menus or dialog boxes appear in **bold**. Here is an example: "Select **System info** from the **Administration** panel."

> **Tips or important notes**
> Appear like this.

Get in touch

Feedback from our readers is always welcome.

General feedback: If you have questions about any aspect of this book, email us at customercare@packtpub.com and mention the book title in the subject of your message.

Errata: Although we have taken every care to ensure the accuracy of our content, mistakes do happen. If you have found a mistake in this book, we would be grateful if you would report this to us. Please visit www.packtpub.com/support/errata and fill in the form.

Piracy: If you come across any illegal copies of our works in any form on the internet, we would be grateful if you would provide us with the location address or website name. Please contact us at copyright@packt.com with a link to the material.

If you are interested in becoming an author: If there is a topic that you have expertise in and you are interested in either writing or contributing to a book, please visit authors.packtpub.com.

Share Your Thoughts

Once you've read *Persistence Best Practices for Java Applications*, we'd love to hear your thoughts! Please click here to go straight to the Amazon review page for this book and share your feedback.

Your review is important to us and the tech community and will help us make sure we're delivering excellent quality content.

Download a free PDF copy of this book

Thanks for purchasing this book!

Do you like to read on the go but are unable to carry your print books everywhere?

Is your eBook purchase not compatible with the device of your choice?

Don't worry, now with every Packt book you get a DRM-free PDF version of that book at no cost.

Read anywhere, any place, on any device. Search, copy, and paste code from your favorite technical books directly into your application.

The perks don't stop there, you can get exclusive access to discounts, newsletters, and great free content in your inbox daily

Follow these simple steps to get the benefits:

1. Scan the QR code or visit the link below

https://packt.link/free-ebook/9781837631278

2. Submit your proof of purchase
3. That's it! We'll send your free PDF and other benefits to your email directly

Part 1:
Persistence in Cloud Computing – Storing and Managing Data in Modern Software Architecture

In this section of the book, we delve into the essential aspects of persistence in the context of cloud computing. As cloud solutions become increasingly prevalent in modern software architecture, it is vital to understand how to store and manage data effectively in this environment.

This part includes the following chapters:

- *Chapter 1, Storing Data: from the Caves to the Clouds*
- *Chapter 2, Distilling the Multiple Database Flavors*
- *Chapter 3, Exploring Architectural Strategies and Cloud Usage*
- *Chapter 4, Getting the Most out of Design Patterns for Data Management in Cloud-Native Applications*

1

The History of Data Storage – From the Caves to the Cloud

Data: a critical, life-changing, and fundamental asset that supports humanity's existence and evolution. For thousands of years (yes, thousands!), data storage solutions have evolved and supported humans by allowing us to "remember" and share knowledge in easy, maintainable, and searchable manners. Data turns into information, which in turn turns into knowledge. The ability to learn from the past and plan for the future is highly influenced by how we manage data in our systems today.

Software engineers are the catalysts of this process: our responsibility is to define and deliver solutions to people's problems through software engineering – solutions that mostly revolve around data manipulation at a large or small scale. Having understood the importance of persistence in software engineering, you're ready to bring your solutions' persistence to the next level.

In this chapter, we will explore the modern era, where databases have become the backbone of our applications and the entire planet. We will cover the following topics:

- Why do databases exist? The history of databases
- Characteristics of Java persistence frameworks
- The cloud's effect on stateful solutions
- Exploring the trade-offs of distributed database systems – a look into the CAP theorem and beyond

This first chapter provides you with an understanding of the past and current states of data storage technologies, before moving on to more advanced topics. This will give you a better foundation to work from. You will learn how data storage technologies responded to the market's cloud-shift mentality. Finally, you will become familiar with practices such as **Domain-Driven Design** (**DDD**), which perfectly ties in with good persistence development practices, and the challenges faced by distributed data systems that await us in a distributed world, such as the CAP theorem.

Why do databases exist?

A comprehensive understanding of databases is impossible without delving into humanity's history. The desire to preserve knowledge throughout time has made writing one of the most enduring technologies, and looking back, it was first used in temples and caves, which can be recognized as the first non-computational databases of humankind.

Today, the industry emphasizes accurate and well-recorded information. As a matter of fact, the result of an increasing number of people gaining access to technology and joining the global network of information is reflected in research that states that the amount of data doubles every two years.

The history of modern databases began in 1960, when Charles Bachman designed the first database for computers, the **integrated data store**, or **IDS**, a predecessor to IBM's **Information Management System (IMS)**.

A decade after that, around 1970, one of the most significant events in the history of databases occurred when E. F. Codd published his paper *A Relational Model of Data for Large Shared Data Banks*, coining the term **relational database**.

Finally, as the next and probably most recent breakthrough in terms of data storage, came NoSQL, which refers to any non-relational database. Some say **NoSQL** stands for *Non-SQL*, while others say it stands for *Not Only SQL*.

NoSQL databases power some of the most popular online applications. Here are a few:

- **Google**: Google uses NoSQL Bigtable for Google Mail, Google Maps, Google Earth, and Google Finance
- **Netflix**: Netflix likes the high availability of the NoSQL database and uses a combination of SimpleDB, HBase, and Cassandra
- **Uber**: Uber uses Riak, a distributed NoSQL database with a flexible key-value store model
- **LinkedIn**: LinkedIn built its own NoSQL database called Espresso, which is a document-oriented database

The challenges of handling data

The evolution of database systems has been marked by key milestones over the decades. In the early days, when storage was expensive, the challenge was finding ways to reduce information waste. A reduction of even one million dollars' worth of information was a significant achievement.

> **Did you know?**
> At the dawn of the database era, a megabyte used to cost around 5 million dollars!
> `https://ourworldindata.org/grapher/historical-cost-of-computer-memory-and-storage`

Today, megabyte cost isn't the challenge anymore as we're living at the cost of 0.001 $/MB. As time passed and storage became cheaper, the methods of reducing duplicate data started to negatively impact an application's response time. Normalization and the attempts to reduce data duplication, multiple join queries, and massive amounts of data did not help as much.

It's no surprise that challenges to this model would eventually emerge. As noted by the esteemed and respected authors of the book *Fundamentals of Software Architecture* (`https://www.amazon.com/dp/1492043451/`), definitive solutions don't exist; instead, we are presented with many solutions where each is accompanied by its own set of benefits and drawbacks.

Obviously, the same applies to databases.

There is no one-size-fits-all solution when it comes to data storage solutions.

In the 2000s, new storage solutions, such as NoSQL databases, began to gain popularity and architects had more options to choose from. This doesn't mean that SQL stopped being relevant, but rather that architects must now navigate the complexities of choosing the right paradigm for each problem.

As the database landscape went through these phases, the application's scenario also changed. Discussions moved toward the motivations and challenges of adopting a microservices architecture style, bringing us back to the multiple persistence strategies available. Traditionally, architectures included relational database solutions, with one or two instances (given its increased cost). Now, as new storage solutions mature, architectural solutions start to include persistence based on NoSQL databases, scaling up to multiple running instances. The possibility of storing data in multiple ways, throughout different services that compose a single broader solution, is a good environment for potential new solutions with polyglot persistence.

Polyglot persistence is the idea that computer applications can use different database types to take advantage of the fact that various engine systems are better equipped to handle different problems. Complex applications often involve different types of problems, so choosing the right tool for each job can be more productive than trying to solve all aspects of the problem using a single solution.

When analyzing solutions in most recent times, the reality confronts us, developers and architects, with the complexity of choice. How do we handle data, having to consider a scenario with multiple data types? To make it clear, we're talking about mixing and matching hundreds of possible solutions. The best path is to prepare by learning about persistence fundamentals, best practices, and paradigms. And finally, being aware that no matter how much we desire a fast, scalable, highly available, precise, *and* consistent solution – we now know that, according to the CAP theorem, a concept discussed later in this chapter, that may be impossible.

Next, we'll narrow down our focus specifically to persistence within the context of Java applications.

Characteristics of Java persistence frameworks

Let's grasp the idea of the differences between the Java language and the multiple databases available. Java, an **Object-Oriented Programming (OOP)** language, naturally offers features such as inheritance, encapsulation, and types, which supports the creation of well-designed code. Unfortunately, not all of these features are supported by database systems.

As a consequence, when integrating both language and database paradigms, some of their unique advantages might get lost. This complexity becomes clear when we observe that in all data manipulation between in-memory objects and the database schema, there should be some data mapping and conversion. It is critical to either define a preferred approach or provide an isolation layer. In Java, the most systematic way to integrate both worlds is through the usage of frameworks. Frameworks come in various types and categories shaped by their **communication levels** and the **provided API dynamics**. In *Figure 1.1*, observe the key aspects of both concepts:

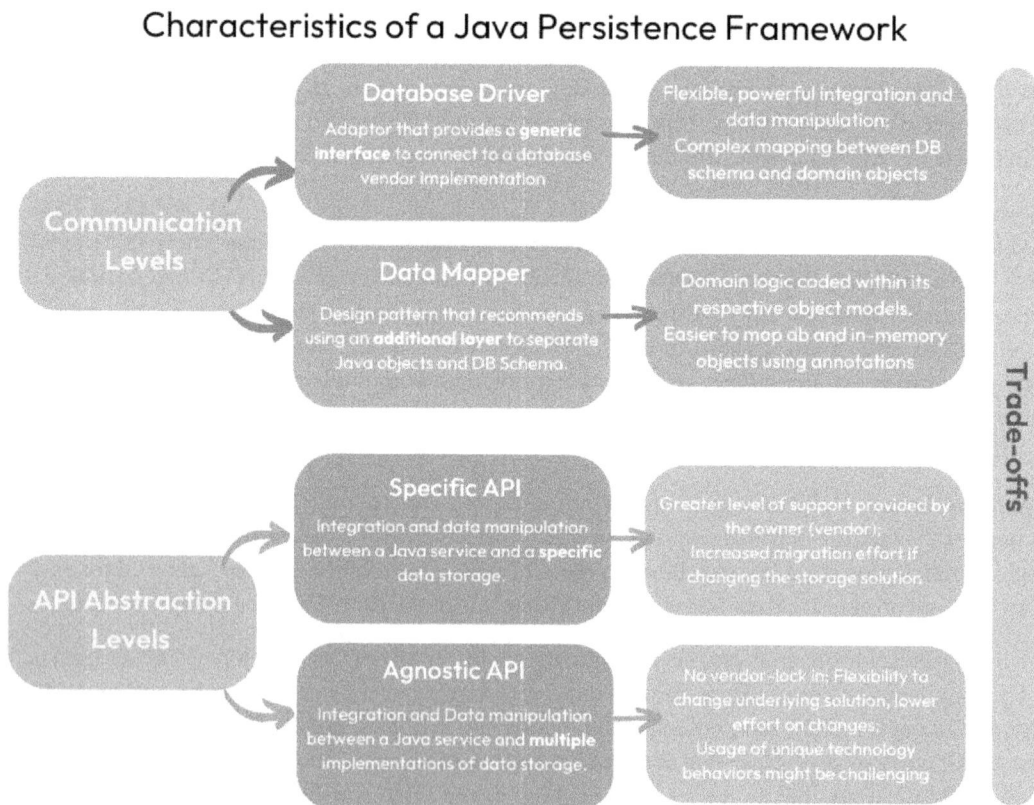

Figure 1.1 – Considerations about the different characteristics of a Java persistence framework

- **Communication levels**: Define how unrelated the code is from either the database or OOP paradigm. The code can be designed to be more similar to one of the two domains. To clarify, take into consideration two common approaches for integrating a Java app with a database – using a database driver directly or relying on the mapper pattern:

  - Directly adopting a driver (e.g., JDBC Driver) means working closer to the database domain space. A database driver that is easy to work with is usually data-oriented. A downside is the need to have more boilerplate code to be able to map and convert all manipulated data between the database model and the Java domain objects.

  - The mapper pattern provides the possibility to map a database structure to the Java objects using the completely opposite approach. In the context of mapping frameworks such as Hibernate and Panache, the primary objective is to align more closely with the OOP paradigm rather than focusing primarily on the database. While offering the benefit of reduced boilerplate code, it has as a trade-off, to coexist with a constant object-relational impedance mismatch and its consequent performance impacts. This topic will be covered in more detail in further chapters.

- **API abstraction levels**: To abstract some level of translation between Java and the database during data manipulation and other database interactions, developers rely on a given Java API. To clarify the abstraction level of an API, you can ask, for example, *"How many different database types does a given database API support?"* When using SQL as a standard for relational database integration, developers can use a *single API* and integrate it with *all* relational database flavors. There are two types of APIs:

  - A specific API may offer more accurate updates from the vendor, but it also means that any solution that relies on that API will need to be changed if you ever want to switch to a different database (e.g., Morphia or Neo4j-OGM – **OGM** stands for **Object Graph Mapper**)

  - An agnostic API is more flexible and can be used with many different types of databases, but it can be more challenging to manage updates or particular behaviors for each one

---

Code design– DDD versus data-oriented

In the renowned book *Clean Code*, the author, known as Uncle Bob, states OOP languages have the benefit of hiding data in order to expose its behavior. In the same line of thought, we see DDD, which proposes the usage of a ubiquitous language throughout the domain's code and related communication. The implementation of such a proposal can be achieved through the usage of OOP concepts. In *Data-Oriented Programming*, Yehonathan Sharvit suggests simplifying complexity by giving relevance to data and treating it as a "first-class citizen."

Luckily, there are several frameworks to assist us in the challenges of delivering performant persistence layers. Although we understand that more options bring back the paradox of choice, there's no need to worry – this book is a helpful resource that software engineers can use to learn how to evaluate multiple perspectives within software architecture, especially the details within the data storage integration and data manipulation space.

So far, we have explored the diverse methods that we humans have devised to address a fundamental issue: efficiently storing data in a manner that ensures longevity and serves as a knowledge base to support our evolution. As technology has advanced, multiple persistence strategies have been made available to software architects and developers, including relational and unstructured approaches such as NoSQL. The variety of persistence options has resulted in new challenges in software design; after all, retrieving, storing, and making data available also went through innovation at the application layer. Persistence frameworks, since then and still today, provide architects with different strategies, enabling designs where development is closely associated with the underlying database technology or is more dynamic and agnostic.

Our next stop on this database historical journey is the cloud era. Let's explore how cloud offerings have impacted applications and the ways and *locations* where data can now be stored.

The cloud's effect on stateful solutions

When it comes to databases, professionals need to have an operational perspective in addition to an infrastructure and software architecture perspective. There are several factors to consider regarding a solution's architecture and the required compliance, such as networking, security, cloud backup, and upgrades.

Fortunately, we can use the help of cloud services. The cloud, as a technology-related concept, has been defined by the **National Institute of Standards and Technology (NIST)** as a model that enables the consumption, on-demand and via a network, of a shared set of computing resources that are rapidly made available.

You might have heard a joke in tech communities that says that "the cloud is just somebody else's computer." However, we believe there's more to the cloud than that; we prefer to look at the cloud as follows:

The cloud is somebody else's problem.

The main goal of adopting cloud services is to outsource non-core business functions to somebody else. This way, we can focus on our core competencies.

> Tip
>
> As you read through the book, you'll notice several acronyms are used. In this chapter, we mostly refer to the following cloud service offering types: **Infrastructure as a Service (IaaS)**, **Platform as a Service (PaaS)**, and **Software as a Service (SaaS)**.

Even though you might feel like cloud services could finally be the solution to numerous technical problems you've gone through, remember that delegated responsibilities and tasks also have chances of going very differently from what you expected – for example, services crashing or costs skyrocketing. Since we're discussing the action of "delegating a problem to somebody else," here are three types of cloud services (three ways to "delegate") and their respective target audiences:

- **IaaS**: *Infrastructure* is not your problem. The target audience is people who work on the operation side, such as SREs.

- **PaaS**: The *infrastructure* and *operation* are not your problems. The main target audience is software engineers.

- **SaaS**: The *infrastructure*, *operation*, and *software* are not your problem. In this case, the target audience is the end user, who doesn't necessarily know how to code.

As we previously pointed out in this chapter, *every solution's trade-offs must be considered*. Picking the PaaS cloud offering as an example: this model offers a higher level of abstraction in exchange for a bit of a higher price tag.

What about cloud offerings for data storage, then? As pointed out by Dan More in the book *97 Things Every Cloud Engineer Should Know* (https://www.amazon.com/dp/1492076732), databases can also be used as managed cloud services. Looking at a managed database service, you could consider that someone else (a vendor) will provide a service to abstract most of (and in some cases, all of) the database infrastructure and management tasks.

Database as a Service (**DBaaS**) is a popular type of cloud service that allows users to choose from a variety of database flavors, running in multiple regions and managed by different cloud providers.

Cloud services can be helpful when we need to explore various architectural persistence solutions and delegate complexity. They have been widely adopted and proven to be effective in serving this purpose.

With cloud offerings and microservices architecture adoption, distributed solutions are becoming more prevalent. Architects then have to handle new challenges related to data integrity and unexpected occurrences of inconsistency in data in applications that must meet such requirements.

Exploring the trade-offs of distributed database systems – a look into the CAP theorem and beyond

If the perfect **Distributed Database System** (**DDBS**) were to be described, it would certainly be a database that was highly scalable, provided perfectly consistent data, and didn't require too much attention in regard to management (tasks such as backup, migrations, and managing the network). Unfortunately, the CAP theorem, formulated by Eric Brewer, states that that's not possible.

> **Note**
>
> To date, there is no database solution that can provide the ideal combination of features such as total data consistency, high availability, and scalability all together.
>
> For details, check: *Towards robust distributed systems*. PODC. 7. 10.1145/343477.343502 (`https://www.researchgate.net/publication/221343719_Towards_robust_distributed_systems`).

The **CAP theorem** is a way of understanding the trade-offs between different properties of a DDBS. Eric Brewer, at the 2000 Symposium on **Principles of Distributed Computing (PODC)**, conjectured that when creating a DDBS, *"you can have at most two of these properties for any shared-data system,"* referring to the properties **consistency**, **availability**, and **tolerance to network partitions**.

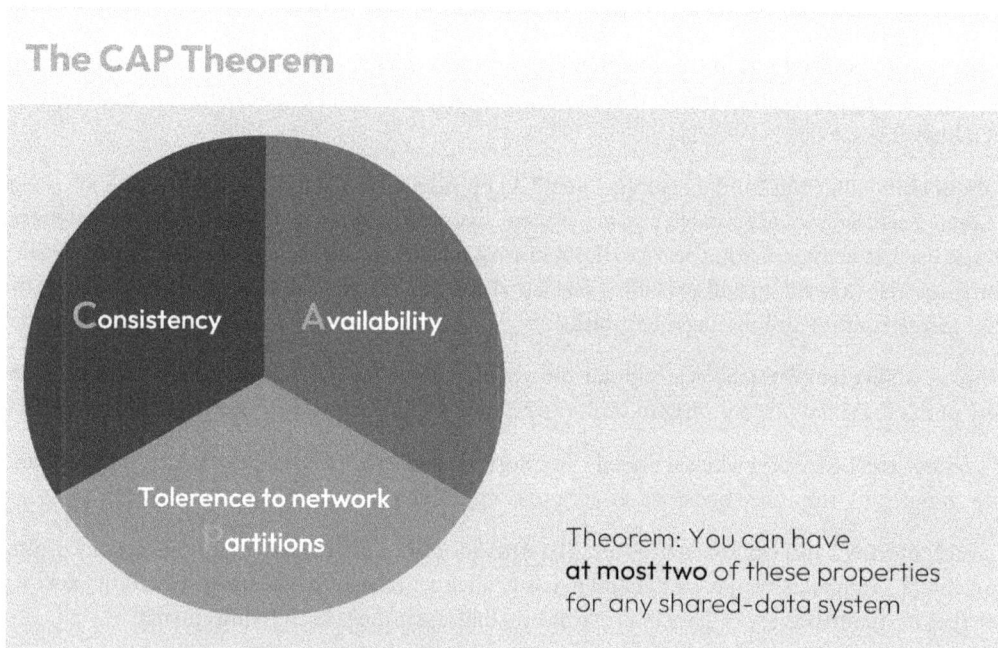

Figure 1.2 – Representation inspired by Eric Brewer's keynote presentation

> **Note**
>
> *Towards Robust Distributed Systems.* For more information on Eric Brewer's work, refer to Brewer, Eric. (2000), presentation: `https://people.eecs.berkeley.edu/~brewer/cs262b-2004/PODC-keynote.pdf`.

The three characteristics described in the CAP theorem can be described as follows:

- **Consistency**: The guarantee that every node in a distributed cluster returns the same, most recent, successful write.

- **Availability**: Every non-failing node returns a response for all read and write requests in a reasonable amount of time.

- **Partition tolerance**: The system continues to function and uphold its consistency guarantees despite network partitions. In other words, the service is running despite crashes, disk failures, database, software, and OS upgrades, power outages, and other factors.

In other words, the DDBSes we can pick and choose from would only be **CA** (consistent and highly available), **CP** (consistent and partition-tolerant), or **AP** (highly available and partition-tolerant).

Tip

As stressed in the book *Fundamentals of Software Architecture: An Engineering Approach*, good software architecture requires dealing with trade-offs. This is yet another trade-off to take into consideration (`https://www.amazon.com/Fundamentals-Software-Architecture-Engineering-Approach-ebook/dp/B0849MPK73/`).

By considering the CAP theorem, we can then apply this new knowledge to back us up in decision-making processes in regard to choosing between SQL and NoSQL. For example, traditional DBMSes thrive when (mostly) providing the **Atomicity, Consistency, Isolation, and Durability (ACID)** properties; however, in regard to distributed systems, it may be necessary to give up consistency and isolation in order to achieve higher availability and better performance. This is commonly known as sacrificing consistency for availability.

Almost 12 years after the idea of CAP was proposed, Seth Gilbert and Nancy Lynch at MIT published some research, a formal proof of Brewer's conjecture. However, another expert on database system architecture and implementation has also done some research on scalable and distributed systems, adding, to the existing theorem, the consideration of the consistency and latency trade-off.

In 2012, Prof. Daniel Abadi published a study stating CAP has become *"increasingly misunderstood and misapplied, causing significant harm"* leading to unnecessarily limited **Distributed Database Management System (DDBMS)** creation, as CAP only presents limitations in the face of certain types of failures – not during normal operations.

Abadi's paper *Consistency Tradeoffs in Modern Distributed Database System Design* proposes a new formulation, **Performance and Consistency Elasticity Capabilities (PACELC)**, which argues that the trade-offs between consistency and performance can be managed through the use of elasticity. The following question quoted in the paper clarifies the main idea: *"If there is a partition (P), how does the system trade off availability and consistency (A and C); else (E), when the system is running normally in the absence of partitions, how does the system trade off latency (L) and consistency (C)?"*

According to Abadi, a distributed database could be both highly consistent and highly performant, but only under certain conditions – *only* when the system can adjust its consistency level based on network conditions through the use of elasticity.

At this point, the intricacies of building database systems, particularly distributed ones, have been made crystal clear. As professionals tasked with evaluating and selecting DDBSes and designing solutions on top of them, having a fundamental understanding of the concepts discussed in these studies serves as a valuable foundation for informed decision-making.

Summary

Any software application relies heavily on its database, so it's important to give it the attention it deserves. In this chapter, we explored the interesting history of data storage, from its early days to the modern era of cloud computing. Throughout this journey, we witnessed the impacts of data storage evolution on the field of software engineering, and how Java frameworks have also evolved to be able to support polyglot solutions. As experienced software engineers, it is crucial for us to understand the importance of data and solutions that can manage and manipulate it effectively.

Adding to that, we discussed the challenges of relational databases, such as data redundancy and normalization, and how NoSQL databases emerged to handle unstructured data needs. We introduced the CAP theorem and mentioned additional studies, such as PACELC, to explain the challenges of implementing distributed data storage solutions.

As we continue through this book, we'll delve deeper into the advanced architectural and development practices, challenges, and trade-offs you must know about in order to deliver the optimal persistence layer for each solution you get to work with from now on, related to data persistence. After taking a look at the history, motivation, and relationship between databases and Java, get ready to explore, in the next chapter, the different types of databases and their pros and cons.

2
Exploring the Multiple Database Flavors

As a system evolves, especially within a microservices architecture, it becomes necessary to implement a polyglot persistence strategy to accommodate the individual needs of decoupled and independent services. This involves examining various options for storing data, including **Database Management Systems** (**DBMSs**) such as relational, NoSQL, and NewSQL databases. It is important to consider the application's use case scenarios for each type of database in order to avoid overengineering the architectural design.

In this chapter, we will delve into the characteristics and advantages of both traditional relational databases and newer non-relational databases. We will also take a closer look at NewSQL databases and their place in the market.

Before delving into the application details, we'll start by familiarizing ourselves with the multiple storage solutions that we can adopt as the persistence strategy of our solutions. The following topics will be covered:

- A look back at relational databases
- A deep dive into non-relational databases
- NewSQL databases – trying to get the best out of both worlds

A look back at relational databases

Relational databases have been a trusted solution for data storage for over 50 years, with widespread adoption amongst worldwide corporations. One of the best advantages users gain from using relational databases is being able to use **Structured Query Language** (**SQL**).

The fact that SQL is a standard query language supported by multiple vendors means SQL code is portable, and the same SQL code works with little or no modification on many database systems. This is a way of assuring vendor lock-in. Other than that, SQL also helps to reduce the cognitive load of having to learn a new language or API, such as Java's JDBC or JPA.

Now, when referring to the DBMS, in addition to a large variety of tools and resources, relational databases also adhere to the **ACID** principles (**atomicity, consistency, isolation, and durability**), ensuring the reliability and integrity of data transactions. These features make relational databases a reliable choice for a large number of use cases. Relational databases have shown extreme maturity, bringing several success cases that cover, beyond the basics, other capabilities such as providing tools for backup, data visualization, and more. It is a fact that when someone who is used to working with SQL databases switches the focus and starts working with NoSQL storage solutions, they do miss all the side-tooling and thousands of instruments available to support them in their daily tasks.

In Java, we have JDBC, and a language we can learn once and write/apply anywhere. The relational database engine is transparent; thus, JDBC and JPA will be the same.

The essential characteristics of these persistence technologies are the properties associated with data transactions: **atomicity, consistency, isolation, and durability** (**ACID**). Transactions that comply with ACID properties have the following aspects:

- **Atomicity**: A transaction is an atomic unit. Either all database operations occur as a unit, or nothing occurs; it is an 'all or nothing' operation. This results in the prevention of partial data updates and potential data inconsistency.

- **Consistency**: The database should be in a consistent state when a transaction *begins* and *ends*. The transaction should follow every database constraint and rule in order to be adequately consistent.

- **Isolation**: One transaction should not adversely or unexpectedly impact another operation. For example, one table insert will generate a table row ID that is used by the second operation. However, we don't want two operations changing the same row simultaneously.

- **Durability**: Upon completion of a transaction, once committed, the changes will remain permanently. This ensures data consistency even in the case of unexpected failures.

As we will learn in the upcoming chapters, Java applications have multiple different strategies to integrate with a database. There are several design patterns related to data integration that can be used to design the applications, ranging from a lower to higher decoupling from the underlying database. The reason we should worry about the capability of abstracting and having a lower effort when switching to another data storage solution is that even though relational databases are very mature, they are not suitable for every use case. Characteristics such as flexibility in data schema, scalability when handling large datasets in the face of a high number of read and write operations, performance of queries on large datasets, and handling hierarchical and other complex relationships during data modeling are examples of points that are usually stronger on NoSQL databases than on relational ones. Now, we should get a better understanding of the multiple types of NoSQL databases and their characteristics.

A deep dive into non-relational databases (NoSQL)

NoSQL databases provide mechanisms for storing and retrieving unstructured data (non-relational), in stark contrast to the tabular relations used in relational databases. Compared to relational databases, NoSQL databases have better performance and high scalability. They are becoming more popular in several industries, such as finance and streaming. As a result of this increased usage, the number of users and database vendors is growing.

In contrast to the relational database ACID principles, in the NoSQL world, the key characteristics are **BASE** (**basic availability, soft-state, and eventual consistency**). The details of each are as follows:

- **Basic availability**: A high degree of replication ensures data availability even if multiple failures occur.

- **Soft-state**: There is no requirement to have write consistency and no guarantee that the replicated data will be consistent across nodes. Unlike in traditional relational databases, changes can occur without direct user input.

- **Eventual consistency**: The consistency can be handled lazily when data is retrieved (read time). In other words, the data will be eventually consistent so that all nodes will have the same data but not necessarily at the same time.

There are many NoSQL database types, each of which is designed to handle a specific set of workloads and data modeling needs. In order to best define which NoSQL storage type to use, we will now delve into it, getting a clearer view of key-value, document, column-family, and graph database types.

After getting a broad understanding of the multiple flavors of NoSQL, you can refer to *Figure 2.5*, presented at the end of this section, to see how concepts can be compared between relational databases and some of the NoSQL storage flavors.

NoSQL database types – key-value

These are the simplest storage types in the NoSQL world. The data is stored as a collection of key-value pairs in a way that is optimized for storing large amounts of data and efficiently handling data search by its key. This database type has a structure that resembles the `java.util.Map` API where values are mapped to keys.

For example, if using such a paradigm to store information about Greek mythological figures and associate them with their characteristics, the data association would be represented as follows:

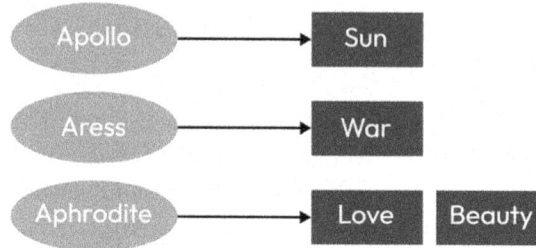

Figure 2.1 – Key-value store database representation

Three Greek mythological figures and the associations between them and their characteristics are represented in the preceding figure. In this example, the value **Sun** has a key **Apollo**, whereas the key **Aphrodite** can be used to refer to both **Love** and **Beauty**.

Currently on the market, some popular implementations of this approach are **Amazon DynamoDB**, **Hazelcast**, and **Redis** databases, the latter two being open source technologies. Each vendor brings its own unique benefits; DynamoDB can be used as a fully managed service, meaning that Amazon takes care of all infrastructure and maintenance required to run the service. Redis is an in-memory database solution that supports pub/sub messaging and caching capabilities. Finally, Hazelcast has support for the MapReduce programming model to perform distributed data processing tasks, plus cross-language support including not only Java but also .NET and Python.

In this database type, there are new concepts to be aware of such as bucket and key-value pair. Although not possible for every single aspect, for those who are used to the traditional SQL world, there are correlations between both worlds' concepts that can facilitate their understanding.

To wrap up, a key-value NoSQL is a database that can store data as a collection of key-value pairs and is optimized for storing large amounts of data and efficiently retrieving it by key. It is known for being easy to use and understand, plus for its horizontal scalability, which makes it a good choice for applications that require high levels of read and write throughput.

Even though there are multiple benefits, key-value databases can be less flexible than other types of NoSQL databases when it comes to data modeling and querying. They do not support complex queries and do not have a rich data model, and can therefore be less suitable for applications that require sophisticated data manipulation. Additionally, key-value databases do not support transactions, which can be a limitation for some use cases.

Now, let's take a look at the document database type and its characteristics.

NoSQL database types – document

The NoSQL document storage type is designed to store, retrieve, and manage documents with a minimally defined structure, such as the XML and JSON formats. A document without a predefined structure, in other words, is a data model that may be composed of numerous fields with different kinds of data, including documents inside other documents. A data structure would look like JSON, as shown in the following code structure:

```
{
    "name":"Diana",
    "duty":["Hunt","Moon","Nature"],
    "age":1000,
    "siblings":{
        "Apollo":"brother"
    }
}
```

The preceding JSON structure shows a document that stores data about a mythological persona named Diana. This same structure holds different data types such as strings, numbers, lists, and other complex objects. Like other types, this is a flexible option to store data in a hierarchical format, *with no need to specify a schema upfront*. Specifically, the document NoSQL database option can be easy to use and require minimal setup, which makes it a good choice for rapid prototyping of quickly developing applications. On the other hand, it generally lacks transaction support and doesn't offer as complex querying capabilities as the complex multi-table join capabilities offered by traditional relational databases.

Amazon SimpleDB, **Apache CouchDB**, and **MongoDB** are all popular NoSQL document-type storage solutions. The former is a fully managed database service offered by Amazon Web Services, while the latter are both open source solutions. All three options offer APIs for interacting with the database using Java.

Having learned more about key-value and document types, let's move on to the next: the wide-column database.

NoSQL database types – wide-column/column-family

The wide-column (also known as column-family) model became popular with the BigTable paper by Google for being a distributed storage system for structured data, and for being projected with the ability to offer high scalability and large storage volume capacity. These databases are optimized for storing large amounts of structured, semi-structured, and unstructured data with a flexible schema, and for supporting high levels of concurrency.

As opposed to other types, data in this type of database is stored in columns rather than in rows, allowing a more flexible and scalable data model. The data stored in a single column family can be of different types and structures, as represented in *Figure 2.2*:

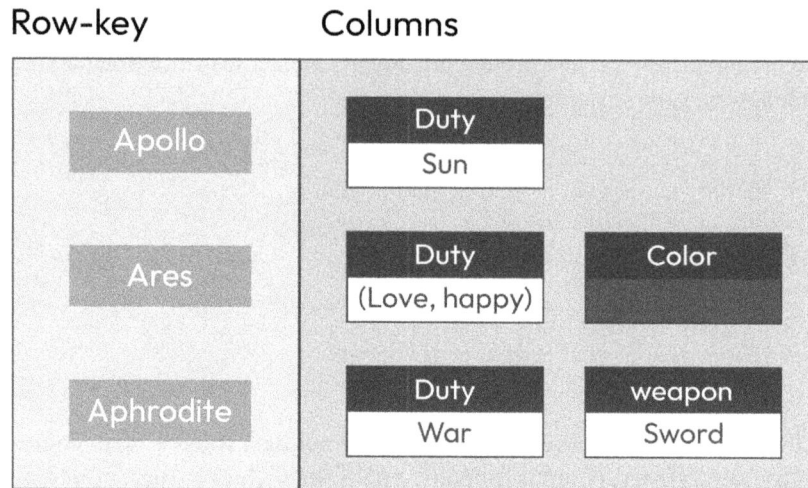

Figure 2.2 – NoSQL column-family type representation

When compared to other NoSQL types, these data can be more difficult to query as they're not stored in the traditional row-based format. Also, the increased schema flexibility represents an increased complexity of tasks such as data model designing and data management.

In regards to engine options, **HBase** and **Cassandra** are both open source, distributed, wide-column NoSQL databases, designed with a focus on handling large amounts of data. **Scylla** is also a distributed wide-column database but is designed as a drop-in replacement for Cassandra and optimized for performance.

In conclusion, wide-column NoSQL databases are powerful tools for storing and managing large amounts of data with a flexible schema, and are very well suited for distributed applications that demand high availability and horizontal scaling storage. However, they can be more difficult to query compared to other NoSQL databases.

Before we move forward to the next section, we will discuss the last type of NoSQL database, which can be particularly useful to complement wide-column databases in certain scenarios: the graph database.

NoSQL database types – graph

The graph NoSQL database type is optimized for storing and querying data with complex relationships. In this approach, data is represented as a graph where the nodes represent entities and the edges represent the relationships between those entities. Observe in *Figure 2.3* the graph structures being used for semantic queries, and the data representation through nodes, edges, and properties:

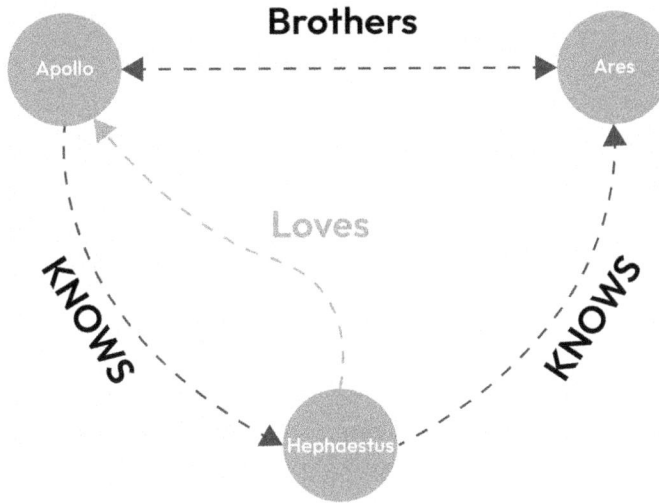

Figure 2.3 – NoSQL graph type representation

The key concepts to be aware of when developing applications that will work with a graph database are as follows:

- **Vertex/Vertice**: Also known as a **node** in a graph. It stores the entity or object data like a table does in traditional relational databases, or like a document does in a document-type NoSQL database.

- **Edge**: An element to establish the relationship between two vertices.

- **Property**: A key-value pair that holds metadata about an edge or vertex element of a graph.

- **Graph**: A collection of vertices and edges representing the relationships between entities.

In a graph, the edge can be either directed or undirected and a direction on the relationship between nodes can exist and, in fact, is an essential concept in a graph structure. If considering the real world, we could compare it to Hollywood stars, for example, where there are people who know an actor but the actor is not aware of all their fans. This association's metadata is stored as part of the edge's direction (relationship) in the graph. In *Figure 2.4*, notice the association direction and type are clearly defined:

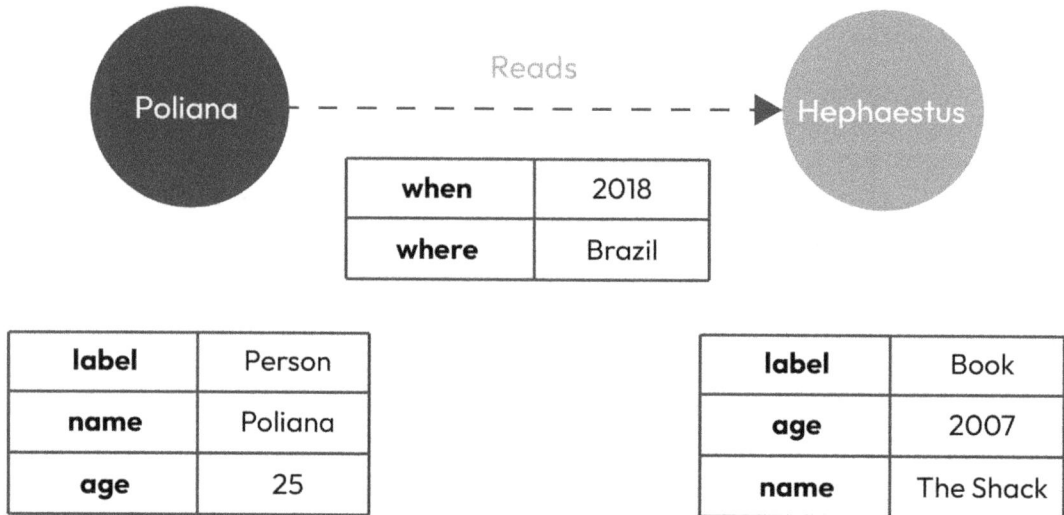

when	2018
where	Brazil

label	Person
name	Poliana
age	25

label	Book
age	2007
name	The Shack

Figure 2.4 – NoSQL graph type data model direction representation

Figure 2.4 shows a directional association going from the vertex **Poliana** to the vertex **Hephaestus**. The association also has its own data, such as **when** and **where** in this case. The direction is especially relevant when querying the graph, as you can't query from **Hephaestus** to **Poliana** – only the other way around.

Graph NoSQL database solutions can fit well in scenarios that require fast querying of highly interconnected data, such as social networks, recommendation engines, and fraud detection systems. Even though they can store and retrieve large amounts of data, that is not always true in the case of large amounts of structured and unstructured data with flexible schema, where the column-family type would be a better fit. Also, complex querying may require traversing the graph in order to find a requested piece of data.

There are several graph database engines to choose from, including **Neo4j**, **InfoGrid**, **Sones**, and **HyperGraphDB**. Each of these engines offers its own unique set of features and capabilities, and the right choice will depend on the specific needs of the application.

We have explored relational databases and NoSQL databases, the two main database storage paradigms in use today for storing and querying structured data using a fixed schema, and for storing and querying large amounts of structured/semi-structured/unstructured data with flexible schema, respectively.

Before moving to the next section, here's a final tip to help you correlate concepts with which you are already familiar with the ones presented so far:

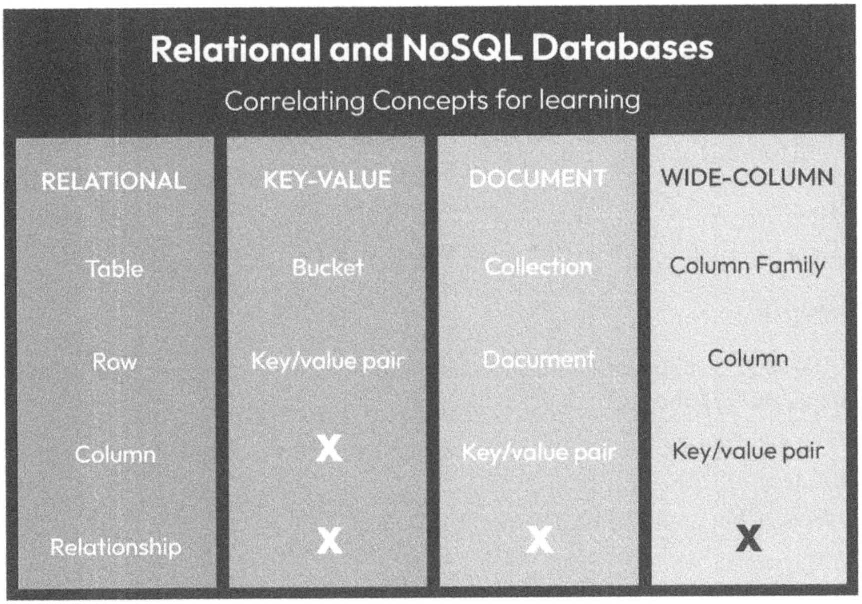

Relational and NoSQL Databases

Correlating Concepts for learning

RELATIONAL	KEY-VALUE	DOCUMENT	WIDE-COLUMN
Table	Bucket	Collection	Column Family
Row	Key/value pair	Document	Column
Column	X	Key/value pair	Key/value pair
Relationship	X	X	X

Figure 2.5 – How concepts can be related between different database flavors for learning purposes

In the next and last section of this chapter, we'll check through a newer category of databases: the NewSQL databases.

NewSQL databases – trying to get the best out of both worlds

NewSQL databases are a hybrid database type that combines the best features of both relational and NoSQL worlds, offering the ability to store and query structured data with a fixed schema while also providing the scalability and flexibility characteristics of NoSQL databases. NewSQL is seen as a way to address the limitations of both relational and NoSQL paradigms and provide a more flexible and scalable solution for modern applications. NewSQL is a database category that aims to unite the best features of both SQL and NoSQL worlds. We have learned two models of consistency: ACID, provided by relational databases, and BASE, by NoSQL. NewSQL seeks to offer a combination of horizontal scalability while maintaining the guarantees of the ACID (atomicity, consistency, isolation, and durability) principles. In other words, it tries to deliver on the guarantees of SQL with the high scalability, flexibility, and performance of NoSQL. Another positive aspect is the ability to use SQL as the querying language.

NewSQL looks like a promising solution, and we can observe (at the time of writing) several relevant companies offering enterprise-grade solutions to the market. It's worth mentioning the involvement of companies that hold immense know-how of both developer and operational needs.

Some examples of NewSQL databases are as follows:

- **VoltDB**
- **ClustrixDB**
- **CockroachDB**

Notice that the NewSQL technology landscape is anything but homogenous, and each solution brings its own advantages and drawbacks.

> **Important note**
> NewSQL uses SQL but usually does not support 100% of it.

Even though this paradigm gives the impression that it may address and solve once and for all the problem presented by the CAP theorem, we should warn you, it does not. Also, generally, hybrid options bring the best and the *worst* of both worlds.

Summary

Database options come in several flavors, and it is crucial to understand the trade-offs with each type. Each data target has specific behaviors, such as SQL having a standard, maturity, several tools, and know-how in its favor. Still, it is pretty hard to work on horizontal scalability.

NoSQL was designed to improve horizontal scalability; however, this came at the cost of less consistency than relational databases are known for.

Finally, NewSQL tries to merge both worlds and bring the benefits of both, but it lacks in both areas.

In the next chapter, we'll cover more about the architectures and strategies of technologies and how to handle them.

Exploring Architectural Strategies and Cloud Usage

In this chapter, we will delve into the topic of architecture from the perspective of services. Specifically, we will explore the relationship between monolithic and microservices architectures and consider the benefits and drawbacks of each approach. We will also examine the use of event-driven architecture as a means of integrating these services. In addition to providing technical foundations, we will aim to provide strategic and contextual insights into how these concepts fit together and why they drive the adoption of various cloud service offerings.

In this book, we will aim to not only provide a solid foundation in technical Java persistence concepts but also offer strategic and contextual insights into how these ideas are interconnected and why they contribute to the growing adoption of various cloud service offerings.

This chapter covers the aforementioned topics throughout the following sections:

- The cloud's influence on software architecture design
- Design patterns – the essential building blocks for software architects
- Monolithic architecture
- Microservices architecture

By the end of this chapter, you will have a deeper understanding of how the overall solution architecture affects data integration design and the pros and cons of using a combination of on-premises and cloud solutions, resulting in hybrid and/or multi-cloud models.

The cloud's influence on software architecture design

While we could start by delving into the specific details of multiple architectural topics – including monolithic, microservices, SOA, event-driven, and event sourcing – we're going to take a different approach. We'll start by providing you with a deeper understanding of these patterns and their importance in software design. Having this background will help to broaden your horizons. Let's explore a few design patterns in more detail.

Design patterns – the essential building blocks for software architects

Over the past few decades, we've identified and shared *"ideas that have been useful in one practical context and will probably be useful in others,"* as wisely said by Martin Fowler:

> *The constant flow of ideas, experiences, and solutions shared by tech enthusiasts worldwide converge into a rich knowledge base that drives and accelerates technological evolution.*

Patterns describe solutions at different levels, from code-level practices to application-level practices. Among the hundreds of patterns out there, we will highlight the practices of design patterns, enterprise application patterns, and software architecture patterns to help us build a solid persistence layer.

The **Gang of Four (GoF)** design patterns and the **Service-Oriented Architecture (SOA)** pattern were important foundations for the more recent Microservices Architecture and Event-Driven Architecture patterns.

Microservices architecture, which has gained popularity in recent years, is an approach to designing and building software systems as a collection of small, independently deployable services. This architecture pattern builds on the ideas of modularity and separation of concerns that were central to SOA but takes them to a deeper level.

People often adopt solutions that they don't actually need because they lack the ability to analyze trends and navigate tech hype. It's important to remember that the goal should be to identify the best solution to a specific problem using available technologies, rather than simply targeting the delivery of cloud-native microservices or other trendy solutions. The key is to understand how to solve a set of business problems using the right technology.

> **Thinking about tech trends – a few things to keep in mind**
>
> A common way to decide whether a specific trend is appropriate for your scenario is to refer to its *technology adoption life cycle*. It brings market adoption insights that help you understand the topic's current maturity; in other words, the more people adopting a specific solution, the more success cases will show up. Not only that but also horror stories, adoption challenges, pros and cons, recommendations, and so on will appear. Looking at the bigger picture, the different maturity groups provide more understanding about the market segments that are embracing the technology.

We now understand that patterns are a set of building blocks that can be used to achieve specific business goals. There are hundreds of patterns covering multiple levels and aspects of application solutions, and new patterns can be derived from the concepts of previous ones. It's important to keep in mind that patterns can be combined and used in different ways to address different goals. For example, a Java service could adopt the repository pattern for its persistence layer, be built on best practices for a microservices architecture, use enterprise integration patterns to communicate with other services, follow the recommendations of 12-factor applications for cloud-native applications, and adopt design patterns for automated pipeline delivery.

With this in mind, let's delve into the pros and cons of different architectural options such as microservices and monolithic apps, taking into consideration fundamental needs and features.

Monolithic architecture

A traditional way to build a solution is using **monolithic** applications, which are large, standalone software systems that are built as single, cohesive units, with all components being contained within a single package and compiled, managed, and deployed together:

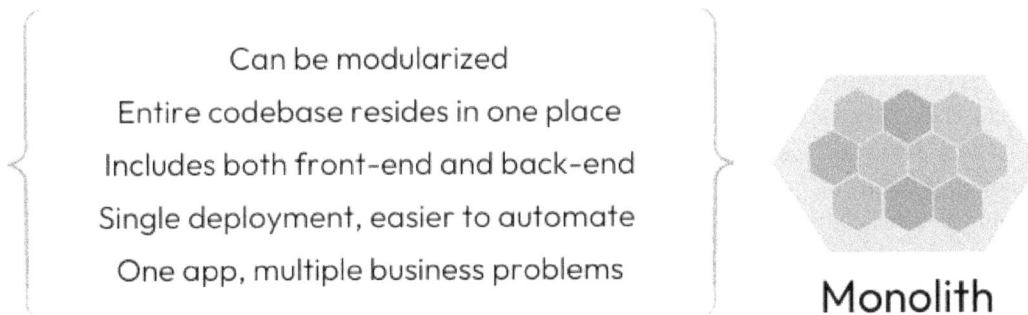

Can be modularized

Entire codebase resides in one place

Includes both front-end and back-end

Single deployment, easier to automate

One app, multiple business problems

Monolith

Figure 3.1 – Monolithic application characteristics

This means that both the frontend and backend are included in the same artifact and must be compiled, managed, and deployed together. While this method can make it easier to initially develop and maintain the application, as the team grows, the maintenance of the code becomes more complex, and deploying updates becomes more challenging and time-consuming.

Performance-wise, scalability is impacted since it is very difficult to upscale or downscale specific features or components.

Defining the relationship between a database and a monolith is not a complex task. Instead of huge databases, some opt to develop monoliths that store and consume data from multiple databases – further increasing maintenance complexity.

Surprisingly, it is possible to create modular applications using a monolithic architecture. Such applications can be designed in a modular fashion, with each module responsible for a specific set of functions and developed independently of the other modules.

Next, to verify its maturity, let's refer to the broad market adoption and feedback. According to trend reports [2] from 2022, the modular monolithic architectural approach has already crossed the chasm and gained widespread adoption among the early majority group.

As with every architectural design, this approach has its advantages and disadvantages. We can analyze the benefits from multiple angles, including (but not restricted to) characteristics such as maintainability, deployment processes and frequency, validation processes, automation pipelines, and others. *Figure 3.2* displays key topics to analyze when designing an app that can result in requiring different levels of effort and cost during each phase of the application life cycle. Some prioritize long-term benefits such as ease of maintenance. Others will prefer to adopt strategies with an easier and faster start:

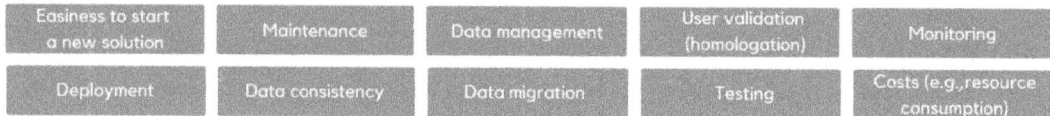

Easiness to start a new solution	Maintenance	Data management	User validation (homologation)	Monitoring
Deployment	Data consistency	Data migration	Testing	Costs (e.g., resource consumption)

Figure 3.2 – Decision points during application design

The best choice will depend on each business need being addressed. In regard to the monolithic architectural style, it is established that its characteristics can represent a significant roadblock for the organization, particularly as the application grows in complexity with multiple development teams and numerous features. Changes and additions to the application in this environment become costly and scaling becomes difficult.

In the face of the downsides of a monolith design inspired by the SOA approach, the concept of microservices comes into play. Microservices propose the decoupling of the components/modules into smaller services, each of which having their own unique responsibility.

Even though microservices involve managing more failure points, a successful implementation allows for benefits such as independent teams, changes, deployments, and scaling of each service within the ecosystem, without affecting the other microservices. This is achieved when maintaining the principle of integrity of each individual service. Let's delve further into the topic and examine the details more closely.

Microservices architecture

Microservice-oriented architecture brings the idea of creating applications decoupled from each other and modeled according to their business domain. These applications are integrated through different protocols, and various communication patterns (REST, GRPC, and asynchronous events, among others) and integration patterns can be adopted. Using a microservice-oriented architecture facilitates quicker and more regular deliveries, as well as introducing a language-agnostic ecosystem.

A microservices architecture has services that are decoupled and independent of other microservices that compose the broader solution. As Sam Newman states in his book *Building Microservices*, there are implicit concepts and behaviors expected from a microservice, as described in *Figure 3.3*:

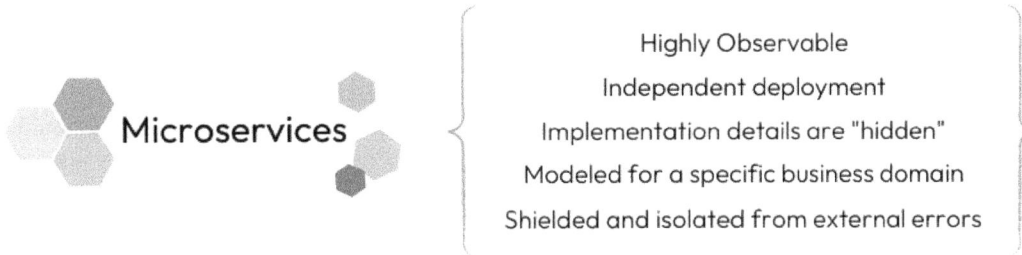

Figure 3.3 – Microservices characteristics

Architects and developers should have in mind not only a core set of characteristics of a microservices architecture but also the critical elements that can result in immense risk to the project, such as the following:

- **Integration latency**: In a monolithic application, the components communicate directly in memory rather than over a network. The result is faster communication compared to the microservices scenario. However, as the number of services and architectural complexity increases, the risk of performance issues and latency increases – potentially becoming a catastrophic problem. To mitigate this risk, take it as a good practice to have proper monitoring and management of thresholds for a service's invocation response time, including the capability of a client service to handle such issues by itself. A recommendation and good practice is to have fault tolerance capabilities in client microservices. For instance, clients should be able to retry previously failed invocations, have proper fallbacks (instead of shutting down due to errors), and be able to reestablish themselves once the requested service comes back to normal functioning.

- **Separation of duties**: Pay attention to the separation of duties of the backend and frontend components. One frontend may depend on multiple backend services. Frontend solutions must be implemented so that, in the event of failure of one of the requested backend services, only the specific associated features have their normal functioning interrupted – all other frontend components should still work properly, guaranteeing the best possible experience possible for the end user.

- **Polyglot environment trap**: The microservice architecture is agnostic to languages and frameworks. Consequently, your environment can become a polyglot. From an architectural and technical leadership perspective, be thrifty in evaluating the technologies to be used so that you don't end up with services implemented with technologies for whose maintenance you lack the required staff. The scope definition and the microservice size should be taken as measures for such definitions.

- **Service size and responsibility**: Determining an appropriate size and scope of a microservice may require the investment of time and effort upfront, at the beginning of the journey to decoupling. Remember to carefully consider the principle of single responsibility (**SOLID**) when measuring a service's scope and size.

- **Forgotten services**: One of the governance challenges is to avoid the existence of orphaned applications in a productive environment. Try to avoid services without owners by establishing a team for each service, including during productive phases. With that, in the face of an unexpected problem or a new change request, it will be simpler to map and define who should be responsible for the tasks.

- **Granular repositories**: Avoid breaking up projects into too many repositories, as this over-granulation can become an unmanageable scenario with more repositories than collaborators in the company.

Common pitfalls of microservices adoption

Microservices architecture adoption brings multiple implications and challenges, and as we should know by now, and as stated in the book *Fundamentals of Software Architecture: An Engineering Approach* (https://www.amazon.com/dp/B08X8H15BW), everything has trade-offs – and *microservices are no exception*.

While initially thought to be a promising approach, the microservices journey has proven to be more complex than estimated by the broader tech industry, especially for small teams. As its adoption increased, we also observed more reports about a range of design issues and missteps. To avoid common pitfalls, it is important to watch out for the following mistakes.

Improperly breaking down domains into microservices

It is very easy to make mistakes when mapping the business problems down to domains, and domains to microservices, especially when starting the move to a microservices approach. This domain leads to solutions that require requests to multiple services to be able to retrieve a relevant set of business data, instead of providing it efficiently through a single request. In other words, regarding data retrieval and querying, an incorrect scope definition can lead to complex code implementation and poorly performing solutions.

Here are some pointers to help guide you find the right path:

- Stakeholders and business experts are involved in the process of domain definition as they can give helpful inputs concerning domain boundaries

- Microservices should have well-defined scope; be responsible for one "thing" and be able to do it well; have functionalities that easily fit together (in other words, that are cohesive); be independently deployable and scalable; and keep in mind that a monolith has higher chances of being more performant since processing happens all in memory, without extra network latency added during microservices integration

Generally speaking, cross-domain services integration can rely on multiple strategies, such as the following:

- Usage of an API gateway to route requests back and forth and filter, transform, and aggregate requested data from multiple sources in one client request

- Data denormalization across services which may result in data duplication in exchange of more efficient data retrieval and querying, relying on techniques such as event-driven architecture to reduce the number of requests needed to retrieve data, or, having event-driven services that can asynchronously filter, aggregate, enrich and provide access to relevant data

Automation gap

As development teams are broken down into smaller and more numerous groups, they start delivering more services, more frequently. The operations of these services' life cycle shouldn't obstruct their potential fast-paced evolution. **Continuous Integration and Continuous Deployment (CI/CD)** is a best practice for microservices and is essential for managing multiple services deployed across multiple deployment environments, ranging from on-premises machines to cloud services.

Adopting as many languages and technologies as teams desire

Deciding on programming languages is certainly one of the most intriguing topics. Even though programmers love to brag about programming languages that allow them to write ultra-short "Hello World" examples and base their decisions on this type of argument, to this day, we have not come across a single project that had a core business goal to output text into some sort of console, terminal, or even write HTML.

A critical decision such as the programming language of a service should not be solely based on the number of lines or the line simplicity of a sample.

An application must become a microservice because it is big

Kindly realize that not every large application *needs* to be a microservice. Here's an interesting metric we'd like you to be familiar with: *cost per line of code.*

(`https://medium.com/swlh/stop-you-dont-need-microservices-dc732d70b3e0`).

The cost mentioned in the link includes computational resources and manpower, including potential changes the organization processes will go through, and potential new software solutions such as containers and container orchestrators.

Different from its counterpart, the monolith, in a microservices architecture, the smaller its code size, the higher the *cost per line of code*, as everything and everyone involved in the service's existence is still required. Sadly, a successfully delivered microservice is only one part of what's needed to solve the actual business problem.

Not taking the best out of independent microservices scaling

Scalability is one of the key advantages of microservices. However, it's important to consider whether it makes sense to scale a component individually. In some cases, it may be more effective to scale the entire system together. Think about it: would it make sense to exclusively scale up unique, smaller parts of the broader solution?

Inconsistent data

Microservices rely on data, and just as with any other distributed database, they're subject to the CAP theorem. This means that whenever you have to update multiple services, you will end up with an added layer of complexity in your application.

One way to work through this is to adopt the SAGA pattern. However, this additional layer of complexity can often have a negative impact on the overall consistency of your data as well.

Beginning with microservices

It's generally a bad idea to assume your project will be based on microservices. This can lead to big problems down the road, especially when it comes to domain definition. Small mistakes can result in several incorrect interdependencies between services and tight coupling. This is why many experts recommend using joins when handling relational data or subdocuments when working with a NoSQL database such as MongoDB.

While joins are a powerful feature in relational databases that allow us to combine data from different tables using foreign keys, they can be inefficient and time-consuming in NoSQL databases, especially for large datasets. This is because joins require multiple queries to be executed and can result in significant network traffic and resource consumption.

In addition, NoSQL databases are optimized for query performance based on the access patterns and usage of the application.

Therefore, it is generally recommended to model the data to minimize the need for joins and use denormalization and embedding techniques to combine related data into a single document.

However, there may be some cases where joins are necessary for NoSQL databases. In those cases, NoSQL databases offer different ways to perform joins, such as using `$lookup` in MongoDB or MapReduce, designed to work more efficiently with the NoSQL data model.

> **Tip – references for common mistakes when adopting microservices**
>
> There's no need to feel discouraged by the challenges presented here; when the architecture is used correctly and in favorable scenarios, it fits perfectly. The point is, *there is no Holy Grail or silver bullet*.
>
> If you want to keep on learning about common mistakes when adopting microservices, refer to the following reading recommendations: Ebin John's *Stop, you don't need microservices* (`https://medium.com/swlh/stop-you-dont-need-microservices-dc732d70b3e0`) and *Should I use Microservices?* by Sam Newman (`https://www.oreilly.com/content/should-i-use-microservices/`).

We have so far outlined the concepts of monolithic and microservices architecture, explored the three main cloud delivery models, IaaS, PaaS, and SaaS, and learned that they can be combined to best fit an organization's needs.

Next, let's expand on cloud deployment models and how having multiple cloud deployment options can help teams to shorten development cycles, fill knowledge gaps, and allow teams to apply their knowledge and effort more productively.

Cloud deployment strategies that favor modern stateful solutions

A cloud deployment model allows applications to rely on an infrastructure that has on-demand usage, elasticity, resiliency, measured access, and other fundamental aspects. Let's have a look at deployment model strategies, such as public and private clouds, how to derive two combinations of them through the hybrid and multi-cloud models, and how best to leverage the available cloud deployment strategies to deliver stateful applications efficiently.

Why the hybrid and multi-cloud models matter

In the search for better flexibility, access to vendor-specific capabilities, integration options, and cost reduction, combinations of cloud deployment models have started to be used more frequently. Organizations have started to combine public and private deployment models and benefit from both private cloud with public cloud services, with a **hybrid cloud** model. Another strategy used is the **multi-cloud** model, which isused when there's a need to run or consume the same service type from different vendors.

When you combine both public and private clouds and leverage similar cloud services from multiple vendors, you are then working with a **hybrid multi-cloud deployment model**.

> **Note**
> Note that the best deployment model isn't the one with the highest number of words in its name – the best model is the one that solves your organization's existing problems.

What with the amount of different technologies and solutions out there, it is natural that teams won't be able to build expertise in every single technology. The fact that it is hard to build a suitably diverse team – in terms of expertise – results in one of two possibilities: a poorly managed and maintained underlying persistence infrastructure or a restricted set of options to be used by developers.

Since data management is such a business-critical component, it shouldn't be overlooked. That is where we can relate to our cloud story: *would it be possible for our business to delegate the management of data storage responsibility to someone else?* At this point, we understand that hybrid and multi-cloud models can provide the easy scaling up and down of several types of cloud computing resources. *If only we had a database with such capabilities…*

It turns out we do have one – it is called **Database as a Service** (**DBaaS**).

Besides being able to get everything up and running quickly, using DBaaS, it is possible to delegate complex tasks such as monitoring, version maintenance, security patches maintenance, disaster recovery, and backup. Beyond that, it makes it possible to adopt data storage technologies for which there are no specialized professionals in the team yet, facilitating the freedom of choice to pick the best solution for each scenario. However, if there's a need to directly access the servers that are running the databases or have full control over sensitive data being transferred and stored, DBaaS is not a viable solution. Examples of DBaaS offerings available in the market today are Amazon RDS, AWS Aurora MySQL, Microsoft Azure SQL Database, ScyllaDB, and MongoDB Atlas.

And this is where you get the best of both worlds when architecting solutions: by using decoupled and independent services, you can rely on public cloud services such as DBaaS offerings where they fit, exclusively for the particular services in need, and rely on on-premises data storage solutions for the services that can't deal with the disadvantages of a public cloud offering.

With distributed services across these different deployment models, services integration is a critical architectural aspect to consider.

Distributed systems and their impact on data systems

Microservices are small pieces of a big puzzle: each piece can only serve its true value once the whole puzzle is put together. The qualities of reliability, resiliency, and scalability should not be catered to at each individual service level, but actually, for the proposed integration solution; after all, we agree with Martin Fowler's idea that integration should be treated as strategic to businesses.

"A microservice-based solution's performance is only as good as the ability of its individual components to communicate efficiently."

Example – architecting a food delivery solution

In distributed architectures, handling data integration across services can be difficult. Therefore, we are about to explore architectural concepts and mistakes around integration through a simple example – a microservice-based solution for a food delivery website. Narrowing down the scope, the discussion takes into consideration the following:

- The microservices backend layer
- The microservices data storage
- The cross-services integration

Next, let's look at how the solution is initially drafted as a microservice architecture, and how the integration of these services can highly affect data management and consistency across services.

The basic scenario

In the early development phases, it may look like a non-problematic scenario. For the food delivery example, picture a solution, represented in *Figure 3.4*, composed of four microservices, each backed by its persistence and data storage strategy: **Order Service**, **Payment Service**, **Kitchen Service**, and **Delivery Service**. The figure represents the microservices, each with its own persistent storage.

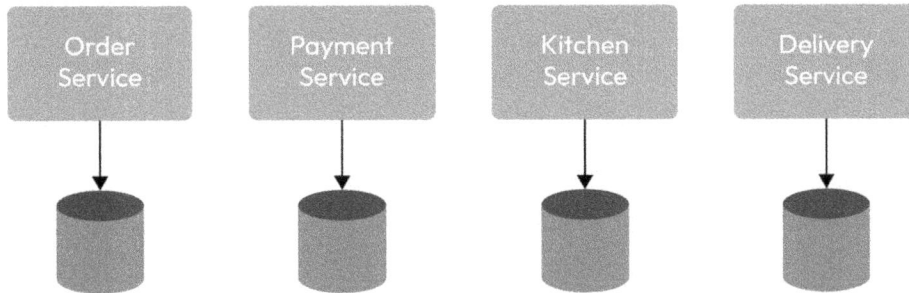

Figure 3.4 – Food delivery service's representation

The happy path of this sample is this: whenever a customer creates and pays for a new *order*, the kitchen cooks it and sends it over to the delivery team, which in turn delivers the order to the customer. *Figure 3.5* demonstrates the new-order process from creation to delivery, where the business flow is processed across the four independent microservices.

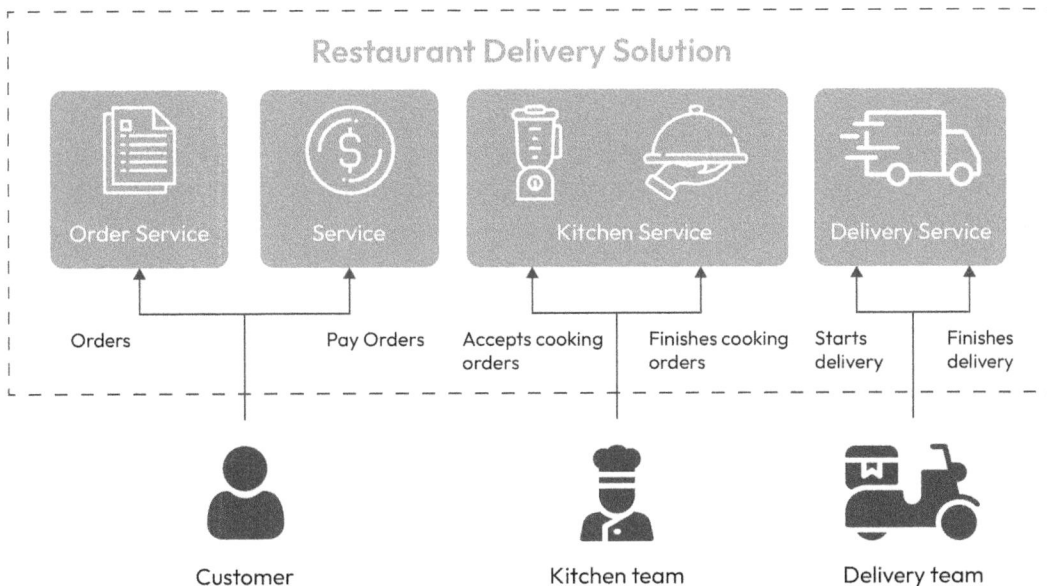

Figure 3.5 – Food delivery business's requirements

From a technical standpoint, this business requirement can be described as follows:

1. **Order Service**: Registers a new order 0001

2. **Payment Service**:

    I.   Registers the required payment for order 0001

    II.   Registers a successful payment of order 0001

3. **Kitchen Service**:

    I.   Notifies incoming order 0001

    II.   Registers that order 0001 is being prepared

    III. Registers that order 0001 is ready for delivery

4. **Delivery Service**:

    I.   Notifies that order 0001 is ready to go to its customer

    II.   Registers delivery of 0001 as completed

To grasp the nuances of this seemingly straightforward business requirement, we must go into the technicalities and explore the various obstacles and potential solutions.

Could this solution be a monolith? Yes, it could. However, delivery services, especially those that are spread across multiple customers/order providers/delivery providers, are built on an extensive list of business needs not covered in a simple example used for learning purposes. The architectural solutions for and business needs of real-world delivery services such as Uber Eats and DoorDash are good examples of complex, real-world scenarios.

This solution's microservice has an independent database, which not only aligns with the microservice's ideas but also brings a good level of encapsulation and reduces the number of errors caused by changes (e.g., schema changes).

The challenges of integrating services around a central piece of data

Even though all four services are designed to be *independent*, they all function around one key feature: the *order*. And a problem regarding this data appears: *how do you manage and handle order data across the four services*?

Microservices' shared database

Some could leverage data storage as the integration layer for these services, having a single schema holding not only the order details but also the payment, kitchen, and delivery information as well.

Unfortunately, this is an inadvisable solution known as shared databases (a.k.a. integration databases). *Figure 3.6.* shows that in this case, all services rely on a single schema to maintain an order's information:

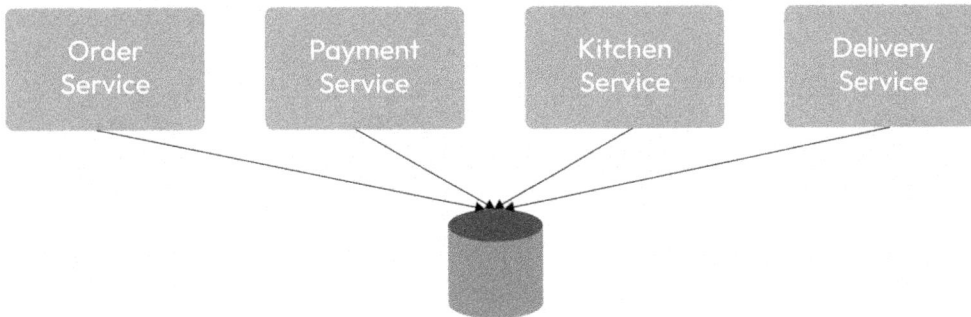

Figure 3.6 – Shared database anti-pattern

In the preceding example, a service implementation may look simple since it doesn't have to handle integration aspects. However, multiple problems were added to the solution, and design principles were broken:

- Microservices should be decoupled and independent.
- Bottlenecks and performance impacts, as well as unexpected exceptions such as lock exceptions.
- Involvement of multiple business areas since bounded contexts are not respected.
- Changes to the database may require changes to all services.
- Multiple services acting on the same data might lead to inconsistency.
- Higher risk of bugs and errors. For instance, a change made to one service that is not expected by all other services.

Considering the aforementioned problems and many more, it becomes easy to see that this is not a good route.

Dual-write anti-pattern

Trying to avoid the aforementioned problems, we might consider having independent services, each with its respective database. However, in this solution, services do not maintain a copy of the order on their databases, but they should also update the order status both in their databases and in the order service's database.

In *Figure 3.6*, observe that the order service is independent and maintains order data in its data storage. However, other services rely on replicating order data in their own databases and maintaining an order's status in both databases – their own and the order service's:

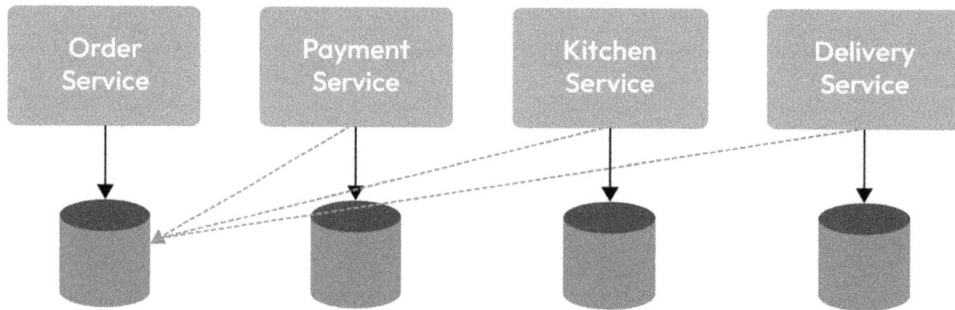

Figure 3.7 – Dual-write anti-pattern

And this, dear reader, is yet another anti-pattern: the *dual-write* anti-pattern. It brings high chances of ending up with inconsistent data and integrity issues, as it is not possible to ensure that both writes will complete successfully or none at all, as in a single transaction. It's a common mistake in scenarios such as handling distributed data systems, using exclusive data storage for analytics, implementing dedicated search index tools, and designing event-driven solutions (e.g., writing the same data to a database and Kafka).

Right upfront, we've highlighted two red flags for distributed architecture regarding data access and management:

- The first is that a service should not directly change any data owned and consumed by another service, as represented by the arrows in *Figure 3.7*, where all services are modifying data in the order service's database

- The second is that one service should *not* be responsible for, or act upon, the manipulation and maintenance of data persistence and consistency across multiple data storage solutions, including not only cross-services as shown in *Figure 3.5* but also between different data storage types as exemplified in *Figure 3.6*

Both anti-patterns, as well as use cases and potential solutions and strategies for data integration, are explored in great depth in *Chapter 10* and *Chapter 11*. For now, it is enough to have the awareness that *there are anti-patterns in distributed data service integration* that can result in performance bottlenecks, data inconsistency, and reliability loss.

At this point, we can better comprehend why integration shows itself as a crucial architectural aspect for delivering modern microservices-based solutions. Next, let's take a look at another way to integrate distributed services by relying on event-driven architecture for asynchronous data integration.

Unveiling change data capture for data integration

Services integration can be synchronous or asynchronous and can use different mechanisms and take different forms, such as file-based, shared database, message-based, API-based (e.g., REST, SOAP), event-driven, and many more. For the purposes of this book, we will consider aspects of **Event-Driven Architecture (EDA)**, as it enables the usage of data integration patterns such as **change data capture**.

Technologies around event-driven patterns were created to allow databases – even traditional ones – to have a new capability: emit events. You read that correctly; it is possible for traditional relational databases (and other databases as well) to go beyond the basics and allow developers to rely on Change Data Capture.

With Change Data Capture, database operations can be captured and emitted as events by a component external to the database and microservices of the solution. With this, developers are able to create event-driven services that can then react and respond to the aforementioned data events, or "notifications."

As you might have expected, EDA is not all sunshine and roses. Understanding what's happening throughout a single business flow can be quite overwhelming in this architectural style when multiple services and a high number of events are involved. Troubleshooting can also be extremely complex since the tracking process isn't linear and does not happen in unique transactions. When working with EDA, forget about automatic rollbacks.

Even though each of the mentioned challenges can be addressed or mitigated, notice these are only some of the items in a list of potential drawbacks for EDA; therefore, don't forget to do your evaluations for the scenario in question, and validate whether EDA is the best solution for it or not.

Knowing the integration benefits offered by EDA is crucial to integrating your services without breaking patterns, best practices, and recommendations, and is critical to ensuring that you reap the benefits of asynchronous, highly scalable integration.

Summary

At this point, we have examined the influence of cloud technology on software architecture design and the importance of design patterns as building blocks for software architects. We compared monolithic and microservices architectures, shedding light on their advantages and disadvantages.

We also explored cloud deployment strategies such as hybrid and multi-cloud models, and how these strategies, combined with managed services such as DbaaS, can speed up the development and delivery of stateful solutions. On the other hand, we also discovered that how we integrate data in distributed systems can impact data management and usage directly. When integrating distributed stateful service, we now know we must be cautious about using anti-patterns such as shared databases and "dual-writes".

At the end of the chapter, we unveiled the potential of Change Data Capture for data integration in EDA, which increases architectural complexity (more components and technologies) in exchange for a completely decoupled and asynchronous integration.

After discussing architectural and deployment model choices, we will next dive deeper into leveraging design patterns for data management in cloud-native applications, building upon the foundations laid in this chapter.

4
Design Patterns for Data Management in Cloud-Native Applications

Regardless of whether the principles of monolithic or microservices architecture are chosen, we should certainly expect to enhance each service's quality by incorporating yet another software design pattern – the **layered architecture** software design pattern. Recently, the term cloud-native has become quite popular and much discussed, describing a set of best practices for optimizing an application in the cloud through the use of containers, orchestration, and automation.

This approach recommends service design and organization in distinct layers, each owning specific responsibilities and well-defined interfaces. The potential guarantee of better abstraction and isolation characteristics is the payoff for the required extra source code and its aggregated code design complexity.

In exploring the reasons why a layered architecture pattern is crucial to healthy applications, particularly concerning persistence integration and data manipulation, this chapter will prepare and guide you throughout a service's design transformation journey. You'll start off by getting familiar with a set of key application-layer design strategies, which will technically explain and demonstrate how an unstructured application, without any level of abstraction, can be transformed into an elegantly designed service, composed of an appropriate set of layers able to provide decent separation and segregation between the persistence implementation technicalities and business context.

Throughout a comparative analysis of each layer design strategy, we will discuss the gains and losses of mistakenly bringing the core ideals to an extreme. On top of the aforementioned solid background, you'll learn through detailed code samples the *reason* for each layer's existence and be able to determine *when* the circumstances present you with an excellent opportunity to use them.

The quality of persistence solutions is right at the core of this chapter's motivation. As previous chapters focused on the broader solution's architecture, integration, and deployment models, we should take a closer look into implementing individual services. We need to take into consideration the powerful outcomes of combining data-related patterns with other popular practices such as **domain-driven**

design (**DDD**). And finally, but no less importantly, we *must* discuss a framework's quality; after all, most Java solutions strongly depend on frameworks. We must, and in this chapter will, shed light on actual framework implementation strategies, to the point of evaluating the impacts of certain frameworks' characteristics such as being built as a reflection or reflectionless technology.

The content is broken down and discussed throughout the following sections:

- Design patterns applied to the Java persistence layer
- Navigating the Java mapping landscape – evaluating framework trade-offs
- Data transfer between the view and underlying layers

Technical requirements

- Java 17
- Maven
- A Git client
- A GitHub account

The code samples demonstrated are available at `https://github.com/PacktPublishing/Persistence-Best-Practices-for-Java-Applications/`.

Design patterns applied to the Java persistence layer

We, as software engineers, often discuss and adopt layered architectural solutions, but why? Why should we consider using this code style? What are its surrounding trade-offs? In order to provide a better understanding of code design patterns, we'll illustrate a scenario around accomplishing a simple mission: storing and retrieving data from a database – more specifically, a library system that manages books and their respective data. At first glance, our task looks quite straightforward, right? Let's get started.

First, we see the need to create an entity, a `Book` class, which we can use to handle the library's domain – our business domain. The first characteristic we can assume is that our `Book` entity should be **immutable**. In this domain, the `Book` entity attributes should be `title`, `author`, `publisher`, and `genre`.

The following code sample represents the described `Book` class. Notice all fields are set as `final` to implement the immutability assumption. To enable developers to create instances of this class, the `Book` class brings a `constructor` method and a `builder` class (*removed for brevity*):

```
public class Book {
    private final String title;
    private final String author;
    private final String publisher;
```

```
    private final String genre;
    // constructor method
    // builder inner class
}
```

The first entity, Book, is implemented as an immutable class.

The instance variables are set as final. Therefore, it is not possible to change the value of them after the object is initialized. Notice as well that there are no setter methods. If you are interested in the detailed implementation of the inner class, refer to the Book class (https://github. com/architects4j/mastering-java-persistence-book-samples/blob/ e594bb17eab3dc97665b495b4245312bfd0f421b/chapter-04/src/main/java/ dev/a4j/mastering/data/Book.java#L14-L66) implementation.

To simulate the serialization from and to the database, we'll use the db in-memory object of type Map of Map: Map<String, Map<String, Object>> db:

```
import java.util.HashMap;
import java.util.Map;
import java.util.Objects;
import java.util.Optional;

public enum Database {

    INSTANCE;
    private Map<String, Map<String, Object>> db = new
      HashMap<>();


    public Optional<Map<String, Object>> findById(String id) {
        Objects.requireNonNull(id, "id is required");
        return Optional.ofNullable(db.get(id));
    }

    public Map<String, Object> insert(String id,
      Map<String, Object> entry) {
        Objects.requireNonNull(id, "id is required");
        Objects.requireNonNull(entry, "entry is required");
        db.put(id, entry);
        return entry;
    }

    public void delete(String id) {
        Objects.requireNonNull(id, "id is required");
        db.remove(id);
```

```
    }

    public Map<String, Object> update(String id,
      Map<String, Object> entry) {
        Objects.requireNonNull(id, "id is required");
        Objects.requireNonNull(entry, "entry is required");
        if (findById(id).isEmpty()) {
            throw new IllegalArgumentException("The
              database cannot be updated");
        }
        return entry;
    }
}
```

The memory database is not fancy and does not cover any concurrency cases, but it is simple to put more focus on the layers.

> **Note**
>
> The core example's goal is to assess a database layer, such as JDBC, so we won't cover race conditions and other *real-life* challenges.

To keep our focus on entity mapping and code design, our simulated in-memory *database* exclusively addresses the four **create, read, update, and delete (CRUD)** operations.

Moving forward with the implementation, the next action would be to implement every CRUD database operation. Remember that at our scenario's starting point, we currently *live a life with no layers*; therefore, all our methods should reside in the same class.

Next, we will take a look at the unstructured approach we've mentioned, followed by how it compares to the same solution implemented using the **data mapper**, **data access object (DAO)**, **repository**, and **active record** patterns.

Unstructured code

Our scenario's journey started off with the design of an application with a single layer. This layer is the one the application will rely on for its book data manipulation using operations for inserting a book, converting the underlying representation of a book as a database model from/into a Java domain object, and enabling the querying of a book instance. Well, there *is* good news: we have all we need in a centralized place/file. There should be no surprises or pain when, eventually, there's a maintenance request that requires locating and modifying a database model's field or updating the logic of the entity's method – they reside in the same place.

As this application's capabilities grow and the class gets lengthier, it becomes harder and harder to spot which code is doing what. As we repeatedly noticed happening in real-world applications, unfortunately, such complication eventually and *most certainly* ends up in unnecessary code duplication. This is especially the case for applications with numerous entity classes.

Going back to the code, what follows is a code implementation that instances a new book, and uses our homemade database client to manipulate the book data:

1. Book, Java's domain object, is instanced using CDI mechanisms and its constructor method.

2. The object's attributes are mapped to their respective database model attributes.

3. The database client instance, using CDI, is created or retrieved.

4. The book is saved using the database client's API; the persisted information is composed of the actual Java's model attribute reference plus the manually set database representation, entry.

5. A book's information is retrieved from the database by its ID – title – and stored in the database model representation of type Map – *not the class type* Book.

6. Using a builder, a Book object instance is created from the retrieved data:

```java
Book book = BookSupplier.INSTANCE.get(); // 1
// - - 2 - -
Map<String, Object> entry = new HashMap<>();
entry.put("title", book.getTitle());
entry.put("author", book.getAuthor());
entry.put("publisher", book.getPublisher());
entry.put("genre", book.getGenre());
// - - - -

Database database = Database.INSTANCE; // 3
database.insert(book.getTitle(), entry); //4

Map<String, Object> map = database.findById(book.getTitle())
                .orElseThrow(); // 5

Book entity = Book.builder()
        .title((String) map.get("title"))
        .author((String) map.get("author"))
        .publisher((String) map.get("publisher"))
        .genre((String) map.get("genre"))
        .build(); // 6

System.out.println("the entity result: " + entity);
```

Some might get the impression that this code is simple to handle. However, it is also easy to predict the upcoming impact on long-term support. More code makes maintenance more error-prone, and the result is an application that now represents *risk* to the proper functioning of the *organization* and *business*, not to mention the multiple technical implications.

As software developers, we have likely all encountered (or even designed ourselves) systems that have become increasingly difficult to maintain and modify due to poor design choices. Robert Martin (a.k.a. Uncle Bob), in one of his presentations, named the four signs of a "rotting design" in software: rigidity, fragility, immobility, and viscosity. These four signs are explained as follows:

- **Rigidity**: The tendency for software to change
- **Fragility**: The trend of software breaking in many places every time it is changed
- **Immobility**: The inability to reuse software from other projects
- **Viscosity**: The API making the code harder to hack when we need to change it

Remember we mentioned that duplicates could likely show up in our previous library example? The reason for this is that it's harder to change the code than it is to duplicate it. Predictable results are a breach of the **single responsibility** principle (of the **SOLID** design principles) and a complex testing scenario. After all, how can you stick to the test practices of a test pyramid (see *Figure 4.1*)?

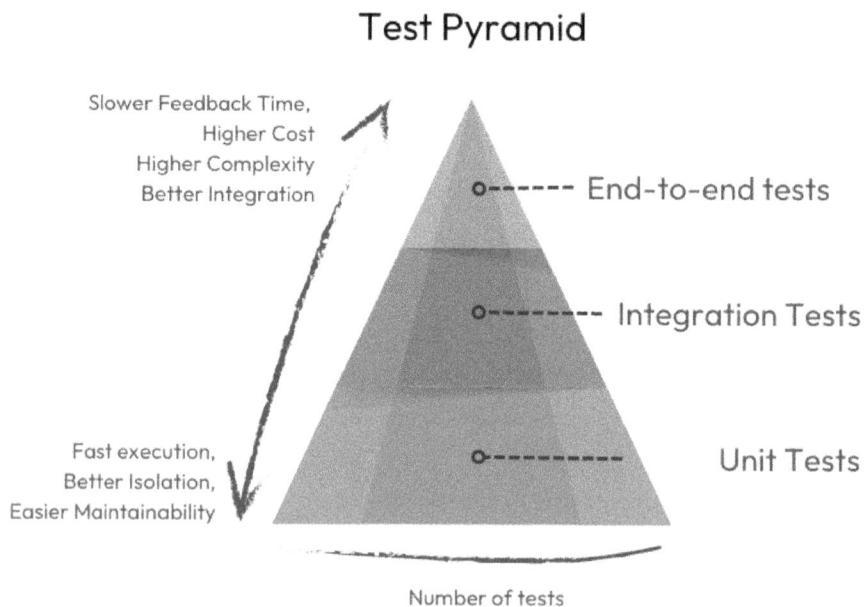

Figure 4.1 – Test pyramid

> **Note**
> We can draft a comparison line between the code design under discussion and the unstructured monolith (see *Building Evolutionary Architecture*); both have a tendency toward increased complexity and hard-to-move architecture – just like a "big ball of mud".

When it comes to persistence, there are a couple more things to consider that we want to highlight:

- The design you choose will impact how much effort will be required when changing between database paradigms. For instance, changing a persistence provider (such as switching from SQL to NoSQL) can be a tough task.

- If you seek to adopt the good practices of the pyramid testing method, having a high coupling between layers makes it hard to accurately write a proper amount of unit tests if compared to integration tests. Have in mind that using a script or a small tool for persistence can be worthwhile in the short term; the problem is that it can also turn into a nightmare in the long run.

- Using more layers can be advantageous. For example, you will be able to abstract away the business logic from the technology specificities. Other than the common **model-view-controller** (**MVC**) basic layers, you can also consider adding an additional layer of abstraction between the model and the database, particularly when working with a three-tier architecture.

Unlike the MVC, which has three distinct layers, in an unstructured code design, the client has direct access to the database. It's not about whether this is a good or bad solution, but rather about highlighting the trade-offs. This approach may be useful when creating a simple/fast migration script or any other piece of code that won't be around for long or isn't expected to grow. The following diagram illustrates this design:

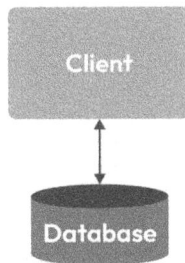

Figure 4.2 – Client-database integration in unstructured code design

As previously mentioned, this model is simple, but as the solution grows in size, we may encounter duplicate code including boilerplate code for converting between the database and the business entity. To address these issues, we will create a first layer to centralize the mapping translation in one place and establish boundaries between the client and the database.

The data mapper pattern

The next step is to create the first layer between the client application and the database. This layer is a great opportunity to reduce the boilerplate and thus minimize bugs – less code, fewer bugs. In the previous example application, you may have noticed that the whole operation of mapping domains and manipulating data is part of a single block, which can make it difficult to read, maintain, and test.

In the book *Just Enough Software Architecture: A Risk-Driven Approach*, we learn about the importance of considering these threats to competent design and using three weapons to combat complexity and risk: partition, knowledge, and *abstraction*.

In this case, we'll use abstraction to hide the technical details and concentrate them in a single place. Here's how we can do that: let's introduce our *treacherous* layer. While a layer can help isolate and abstract a functionality, it also adds more code. This is our trade-off.

The conversion between the database and the Java domain models should also happen, and with more entities, it's going to be even more recurring. In this first step, let's abstract this conversion process in an abstraction layer using the data mapper pattern.

The `BookMapper` class will centralize the conversion behavior in a single place: the layer. From now on, if there is a bug in the conversion, this is the class to check out for any changes in either entity- or database-related code:

```java
class BookMapper {
    private Database database = Database.INSTANCE;

    public Optional<Book> findById(String id) {
        Objects.requireNonNull(id, "id is required");
        return database.findById(id)
                .map(entity());
    }

    private Function<Map<String, Object>, Book> entity() {
        return (map) ->
            Book.builder()
                    .title((String) map.get("title"))
                    .author((String) map.get("author"))
                    .publisher((String)
                      map.get("publisher"))
                    .genre((String) map.get("genre"))
                    .build();
    }

    private Function<Book, Map<String, Object>> database() {
        return (book) -> {
```

```
            Map<String, Object> entry = new HashMap<>();
            entry.put("title", book.getTitle());
            entry.put("author", book.getAuthor());
            entry.put("publisher", book.getPublisher());
            entry.put("genre", book.getGenre());
            return entry;
        };
    }
}
```

As we can observe in the preceding code, BookMapper centralizes the mapping operations of a database model and the application entity model. There are several effective frameworks on the market that can do this type of mapping task, such as the popular option **Hibernate**. These types of frameworks rely on annotations to reduce boilerplate code. Instead of relying on annotations, our mapper class, BookMapper, has a more direct approach: it uses Java functions to encapsulate and execute these conversions.

> **Info – Java functions**
>
> Java functions are a way to encapsulate a piece of code that can be reused throughout your application. They are defined with the public static keyword, followed by the return type, the function name, and a list of parameters within parentheses. Functions can make your code more organized and easier to read, as well as saving time by eliminating the need to write the same code multiple times.

Take a look at how we can use the BookMapper operations:

```
Book book = BookSupplier.INSTANCE.get();
BookMapper mapper = new BookMapper();
mapper.insert(book);
Book entity =
    mapper.findById(book.getTitle()).orElseThrow();
System.out.println("the entity result: " + entity);
```

The preceding sample code introduces the conversion process by using the Mapper class. By doing that, we are abstracting away the conversion operations from this method by moving them to the BookMapper class. Due to the encapsulation, *the client does not know the details of how the translation process is done* – great!

While this is a positive step, there are still improvements to be made as the client is still responsible for invoking the conversion operation. While we can test the conversion process, the high coupling between the client and the technology is still a concern.

To address these issues, our next design includes the addition of a *mapper layer*, which will reduce the friction between the client and the database. This mapper will be used repeatedly, making it a good candidate for a framework such as JPA or Hibernate to operate on.

Overall, introducing this mapper layer will help us improve the flexibility and maintainability of our solution, while also reducing complexity (see *Figure 4.3*):

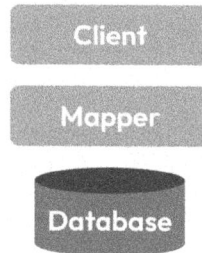

Figure 4.3 – Mapper layer – code design now has an extra abstraction layer

While the mapper layer does make things simpler for the client, it still requires the client to have some knowledge of the database details. This can be problematic as it opens up possibilities for errors when implementing the mapper and its operations. What if we could find a way to reduce this risk? What about creating a new layer, but this time, having it act on the entire database operation?

Let's introduce the DAO pattern! It will allow us to reduce the burden on the client and minimize the chances of implementation errors.

The DAO pattern

The DAO pattern is a way to structure the separation of the application/business layer from the persistence layer. Its main goal is to abstract the whole database operation from the API.

By encapsulating all the operations in a class or interface, the API can be updated whenever needed without affecting the persistence data implementation. This is especially useful in long-term systems, where the DAO implementation may need to be changed.

BookDAO introduces the contracts for inserting and retrieving a Book. As a client of this interface, you don't need to know how it works internally. This makes the code safer by centralizing the database process in a single place. Now BookDAO will be the one working with the database mapper:

```
public interface BookDAO {
    Optional<Book> findById(String id);
    void insert(Book book);
    void update(Book book);
    void deleteByTitle(String title);
}
```

The DAO has an imperative style, which means it's up to the client to define the specific operation. For example, if you are using the API and want to update a book, you must make sure the book exists first; otherwise, you'll get an exception being thrown. If you are familiar with JPA from previous Java EE, you might consider abstracting `EntityManager` in a project such as this. In this example, we'll use the mapper operations in the DAO layer:

```
public class BookMemory implements BookDAO {
//..
    @Override
    public void update(Book book) {
     mapper.update(book);
    }
//...
 }
```

The DAO pattern was made popular by Microsoft in Visual Basic, and later Java through the Sun organization. It was also stated in the early days in the *Core J2EE Patterns* book. It includes the names of the methods, but the goal is to isolate the database with an abstraction, so it doesn't matter whether you are using SQL, NoSQL, or any service.

From a trade-off perspective, we get isolation and better maintainability, and we can test a service unit by mocking the DAO if needed. However, keep in mind that because it's generally an imperative API, it's up to the client to make sure it's using the right method (update or insert, for instance) in the right situations:

```
Book book = BookSupplier.INSTANCE.get();
BookDAO dao = new BookMemory();
dao.insert(book);
Book entity = dao.findById(book.getTitle()) .orElseThrow();
System.out.println("the entity result: " + entity);
```

Using the DAO pattern, from now on, a book client consuming `BookDAO` interacts with books without awareness of the database conversion processes.

By abstracting away the database operations, our client doesn't even need to know about mapping operations, and we can isolate a few things on the persistence side. However, the client still needs to be aware of the data operation. *Figure 4.4* shows the new layer where the client is moved, or abstracted, a bit further away from the database:

Figure 4.4 – Upfront design using DAO pattern brings even more abstraction to the database integration

From the client's perspective, it's an improvement compared to the beginning when the client had to handle the whole process, including the database and entity model conversions, plus the data manipulation operations themselves. But if the client tries to insert twice or update inexistent information, again, we'll get exceptions being thrown. This is a database detail that might not make sense in some cases. So, how can we remove this and focus more on the business? That's what we'll explore in the next section with the repository pattern and the **domain-driven design (DDD)** practices.

Repository pattern boosted by DDD

The repository is a pattern from DDD that focuses on a business perspective and abstracts away storage and infrastructure details. As a client using this API, we don't need to worry about any implementation details. The main focus is on the **ubiquitous language**.

> **DDD and the universal language**
>
> In DDD, the concept of a"ubiquitous language"refers to a shared language that is used by all members of a development team to communicate about the domain model. This language helps to improve communication and reduce misunderstandings by ensuring that everyone is using the same terms to refer to the same concepts. It is an important part of the DDD process and should be fostered and refined throughout the development of a software project.

Going back to our book example, let's start by creating an interface to handle a `Library` book collection. `Library` should be able to save books, find books by title, and when appropriate, unregister books.

The `Library` contracts are going to do the job, and the client won't even know whether the implementation is going to actually insert or update a book. The client's need is to save a book; from the technical perspective, if it's a new book, it's inserted, and if it already exists, it's then updated. The `Library` interface will look like the following:

```
public interface Library {
    Book register(Book book);
```

```
        Optional<Book> findByTitle(String title);
        void unregister(Book book);
}
```

The interface contract uses a ubiquitous language that is closer to the business language and hosts the methods related to its operations. As a client, I don't want to have to care about how the data is stored or where it comes from. If you're a Java developer, you may be familiar with frameworks that implement repository patterns such as **Spring Data**, which uses the `save` method to put away the database operation.

> **Does this framework allow the use of DDD practices?**
>
> Some frameworks use a repository interface methodology, but not all of them follow the DDD practices. You can easily check whether a framework follows DDD practices: look for insert and update methods, such as in the Quarkus framework and JPA with PanacheRepository.

The main difference between a DAO and a repository pattern implementation is the distance, often called the proximity, between the client and the database. While a DAO exposes the behavior of the persistence layer, a repository tends to have a business-oriented exposure.

Our `Library` implementation will use the DAO layer, implemented on the `BookDAO` class. Our DAO already has the mapper conversion operations and database operations ready to go. The following code shows, through the `register` method, how to use the DAO `insert` and `update` methods:

```java
public class LibraryMemory implements Library {
    private final BookDAO dao;

    public LibraryMemory(BookDAO dao) {
        this.dao = dao;
    }


    @Override
    public Book register(Book book) {
        Objects.requireNonNull(book, "book is required");
        if(dao.findByTitle(book.getTitle()).isPresent()) {
            dao.update(book);
        } else {
            dao.insert(book);
        }
        return book;
    }

    @Override
```

```
    public Book unregister(Book book) {
        Objects.requireNonNull(book, "book is required");
        dao.deleteByTitle(book.getTitle());
        return book;
    }

    @Override
    public Optional<Book> findByTitle(String title) {
        Objects.requireNonNull(title, "title is required");
        return dao.findByTitle(title);
    }
}
```

Now, let's take a look at the client code. From the client's perspective, we can notice the abstraction primarily when registering a book – the business-oriented operation named `register` is simplified by delegating the technical decision of updating or inserting to the underlying implementation.

Fameworks and the mapper pattern

There are several frameworks available to help simplify the work of Java developers when it comes to implementing a mapper layer. Some examples include Spring Data, Micronaut, Quarkus, and the Jakarta Data specification.

The following shows the repository client implementation registering a book:

```
Book book = BookSupplier.INSTANCE.get();
Library library = new LibraryMemory(new BookMemory());
library.register(book);
Optional<Book> entity =
  library.findByTitle(book.getTitle());
System.out.println("the entity result: " + entity);
```

By having the preceding repository as the client, there's no need to implement any kind of details on where to obtain this data from. It simplifies and focuses on the business need – registering a book and finding it by its title. However, there's a cost to this. Even when using frameworks, adding more layers also has its trade-offs, such as increased CPU consumption and more locations, which can be potential root causes to be checked in case of eventual bugs. The following figure shows that we've added another layer between the database and the business domain:

Figure 4.5 – Up-front design using repository pattern

Yet again, we have to face the dilemma of software design – where there is no right or wrong answer, just trade-offs. On the one hand, we can move the database as far away as possible and simplify the client implementation. On the other hand, we might go too far and end up tightly integrating the entity and database operations while trying to simplify things.

Our next and final stop on this journey will be the active record pattern.

The active record pattern

The active record is a way to reduce the complexity of using database operations in a model. Martin Fowler defined it in his 2003 book *Patterns of Enterprise Application Architecture*. And here's our next stop – we'll combine the entity with its database operations.

The idea behind this pattern is to use inheritance in Java by having an entity that extends a `Model` class. This gives the entity database capabilities like that of a model with superpowers:

```
public class Book extends Model {
    private final String title;
    private final String author;
    private final String publisher;
    private final String genre;
}
```

But with great power comes great responsibility. One of the main benefits of this pattern is simplicity. If you look at it from an MVC perspective, the model will then hold both business-related logic and data manipulation logic. In our code sample, the `Book` class is able to do several database operations such as inserting, updating, deleting, and finding by ID. The following code shows the client's implementation code, which can create the book and then use the `insert` method:

```
Book book = ...;
book.insert();
Book model = Book.findById(book.getId());
```

This pattern makes sense in certain situations, especially in simple applications. But just as with every other solution, this is not a silver bullet. This pattern has its own concerns, such as breaching the single responsibility principle of SOLID. Some Java frameworks rely on this pattern, such as Panache with Quarkus, ActiveJDBC, and ActiveJPA.

Discussing layers and abstractions can be quite a big topic because the decision you made can have positive and negative consequences.

Now that we've seen different ways to design a persistence integration layer, we will move on to analyzing how frameworks work under the covers and learn which of their characteristics can be weighted when choosing a persistence framework technology.

Navigating the Java mapping landscape – evaluating framework trade-offs

You can now understand the motivations for using layers. It's great that we have a mature Java ecosystem and don't have to do everything manually – *thanks to the frameworks*. Since there are so many of them, we can categorize them based on API usability, proximity, and runtime.

- **Usability:** One of the items to evaluate when looking at a framework is the usability of its API. For instance, you can ask a question such as *"How many times can we use the same API with different databases? Is it even possible?"*

  - **Agnostic API**: A single API can be used with multiple database vendors, types, or paradigms. The positive aspect of this is that an agnostic API reduces the cognitive load since you don't need to learn about a new API for every different database integration. However, you might lose particular database behaviors or have to wait longer to receive feature updates and bug fixes.

  - **Specific API**: The opposite of the agnostic API would be each database requiring a dedicated API – in other words, one API per database. Constantly updated versions are offered to support users to integrate with the latest version of the target database provider. Fortunately, it might have fewer layers and more performance; unfortunately, the cognitive load can be harder to manage when handling polyglot persistence.

- **Proximity**: How close is the framework to the database storage engine?

  - **Communication**: Closer to the database and farther from the domain model; this enables data-driven design, but there might be more boilerplate code.

  - **Mapping**: Closer to the model and farther from the database; this enables DDD and reduces boilerplate code, but being farther from the database can result in ignoring the best practices on the database side.

- **Runtime**: This mainly affects mapping frameworks that rely on annotations usage.

  - **Reflection**: This framework explores the reflection in Java, which allows for more flexibility and variety of runtime plugins. However, the startup time is slower and the application consumes a large amount of memory to execute processes for reading the metadata.

  - **Reflectionless**: This type of framework avoids reflections, making startup faster and more economical. However, metadata processing happens at build time instead of runtime, resulting in longer build and packaging processes, and there is less flexibility for the framework to explore in real time.

In conclusion, there are a variety of Java mapping frameworks to choose from, each with its own trade-offs in terms of API usability, proximity to database implementation details, and runtime capabilities. It's important to consider the specific needs of your project and choose the framework that best fits those needs.

And now that we've split our *all-in-one* class, simplified the client implementation, reduced chances of development errors, and acknowledged the types of frameworks we can pick from the many options available on the market, we can't go forward without discussing the view and controller layers (of MVC) from a data perspective. In the next section, we'll explore how to handle data that travels between the view layer and the underlying layers when using **data transfer objects** (**DTOs**).

Data transfer between the view and underlying layers

In this chapter, we've discussed the importance of application layers for development and how they can impact the maintainability and complexity of a project. We've also looked at the application's model and its relation to the database in an MVC architecture. But wait a moment… when it comes to the view and controller (of MVC), are there any potential impacts on the database integration and its performance?

The answer is *yes*. Let's take a better look at how data transfer from the presentation layer to the underlying layers can benefit or impact your solution.

Most of the time, when developers decide to use the data model on the client side, challenges such as the following can show up:

- **Change-related impacts**: Changes to the model – Book, for example – can directly impact the view layer and require changes to it as well.

- **Security and visibility**: Every aspect of the model will be accessible on the presentation layer. In our Library example, it wouldn't be a good thing to expose sensitive data such as a book's *price*. In a more concrete scenario, suppose you're developing a client consumer of a social media API – it would be unacceptable to find a user by ID, for instance, and expose all non-sensitive and sensitive information, including things such as the user's password! It's strongly recommended to *share only what's necessary – not all information should be visible to the client.*

- **Code evolution and versioning**: In typical scenarios, part of the code is constantly evolving while another part, the *legacy* side, must be maintained. In this case, if a new capability requires changes to the model that is used inside the view layer, it may break the legacy model side of this integration.

- To handle model differences between the old and current code, one approach is to use **versioning**. By versioning the model class used in the view (which is the client), it becomes possible to have the same model offered through different classes and enable the creation of different views, each with their respective adapters.

Given the set of problems in this approach, the conclusion is that the solution to transferring information through presentation layers is to separate the model from the view and controller. That's when the DTO pattern comes into play.

A look back at DTOs

A DTO is a design pattern that facilitates transferring data between a system's layers or components. It can be used to decouple the presentation layer from the business logic, increasing the application's flexibility and maintainability. These simple objects contain data but no associated business logic – they're simple representations of data to be displayed in a view.

The DTOs represent different views from the actual domain models. A DTO could hold, for instance, just the necessary subset of books of information that needs to be presented. In summary, the DTO pattern has benefits such as *model simplification* due to the separation between business and database logic, *performance improvement* since fewer database calls are made, and *enhanced security* by preventing data leaks through the exposure of sensitive attributes.

However, potential drawbacks can also be seen, such as the *higher complexity* caused by an increasing number of layers and classes, the *reduced flexibility* resulting from restricted access to the model's information, which may be needed but not exposed, and the *decreased performance* caused by additional processing on the mapping between DTOs and models.

It's crucial to keep in mind that isolation is key, and too much code can increase complexity and impact performance.

Creating DTOs can denote a lot of work, especially when manually implemented. Fortunately, if you consider the DTO pattern a good fit for your project, there are frameworks available on the market that can make your life easier. Frameworks such as model mapper (`http://modelmapper.org/`) and MapStruct (`https://mapstruct.org/`) can facilitate and speed up the implementation.

We won't go too deep into the presentation layer and the DTO pattern. We want to remind you, though, to be cautious about the view space as well since there are more attention points than simply *persistence* – one example being visualization.

Summary

Layers, layers, and more layers – sometimes, they're excellent allies helping split responsibility, reducing and centralizing the development error risks, and facilitating the adoption of the single responsibility principle from SOLID. Eventually, too many layers can become counterproductive and increase the code design's complexity. When should a new layer be added or removed? The answer will be hidden under each individual application's contextual challenges, technical needs, and business needs.

Through a journey highlighted with code demonstrations, we explored several patterns, from the unstructured and zero-layer application design to the multiple types of multi-tier design adoption and business-oriented simplification techniques. On this journey, we learned about the benefits and drawbacks of using layers to abstract the database from the client in a software application.

Furthermore, we explicitly stated that there is more to the persistence layer for us developers and architects to care about, and that the way we'll visualize and interact with the data on the layer view should also be taken into consideration as a layer that can be impacted by how we design our persistence solutions.

Understanding the application's requirements and context is the key to determining the best patterns to apply to your database integration, and the best cost-benefit level of abstraction and isolation. With that, we're ready to understand and explore the enterprise Java standards made available through Jakarta EE and MicroProfile specifications. In the next chapter, we'll introduce you to two persistence-related specifications that can address multiple challenges mentioned so far, and delve into the power of exploring the spaces of enterprise and microservices Java applications.

Part 2: Jakarta EE, MicroProfile, Modern Persistence Technologies, and Their Trade-Offs

In this section of the book, we explore the intersection of Jakarta EE, MicroProfile, and modern persistence technologies. We dive into the trade-offs associated with different approaches to persistence, providing valuable insights and practical guidance for developers navigating the dynamic landscape of Java persistence.

This part has the following chapters:

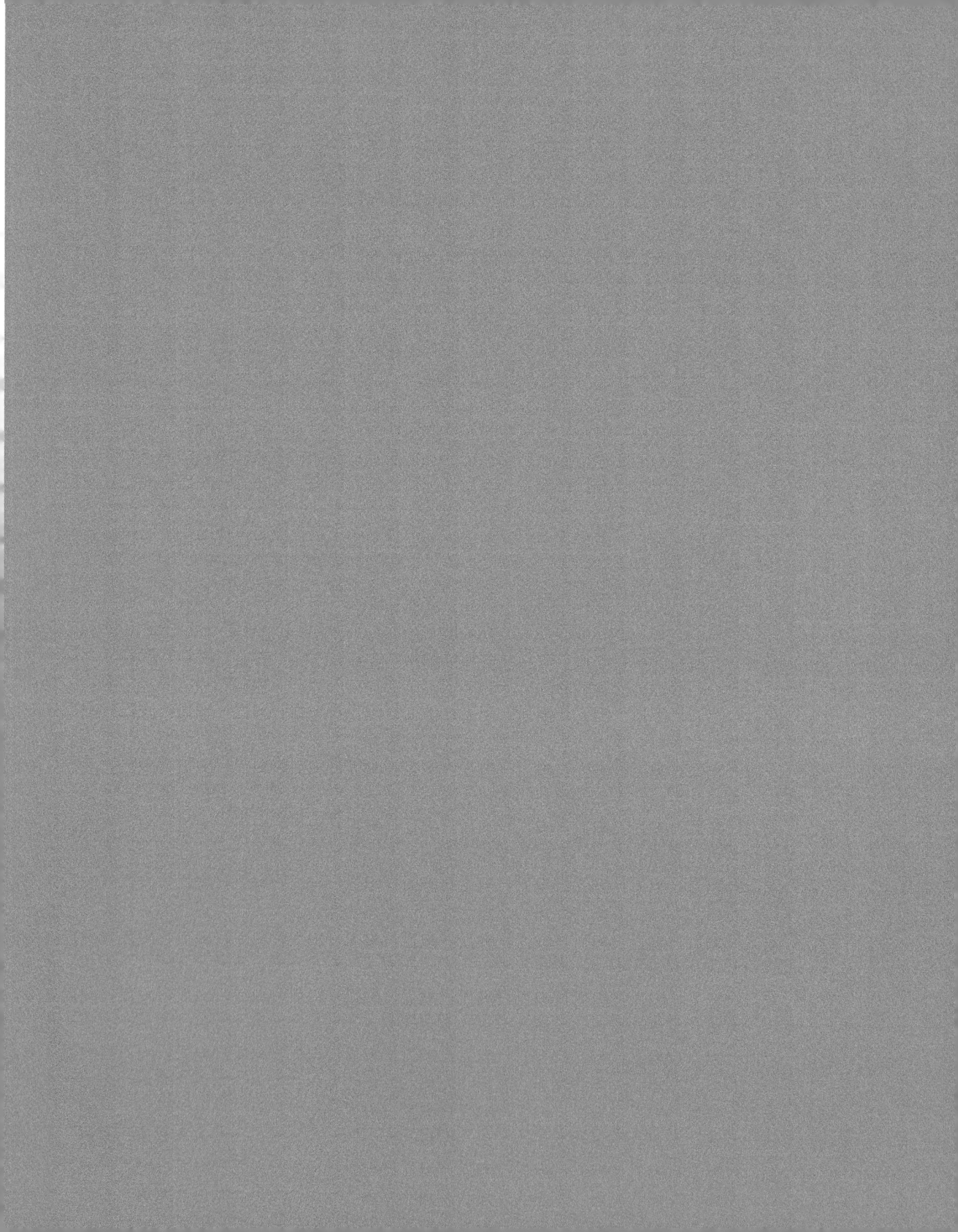

5

Jakarta EE and JPA – State of Affairs

Java, both in language and platform, has improved significantly in enabling an effective developer experience and creating highly performant stateful applications. Remarkable improvements become evident when examining the evolution of Java database integration capabilities and developer experience: look back to the introduction of **Java Database Connectivity** (JDBC) in 1997 with the **Java Development Kit** (JDK) `1.1` and compare it with the most modern experience offered by **Jakarta Enterprise Edition (Jakarta EE), MicroProfile**.

This chapter presents an introduction and overview of the present and future of the main enablers of Java's evolution and constant growth—Jakarta EE, formerly Java EE, and Eclipse MicroProfile. From one side, the Eclipse Foundation and Jakarta EE target enterprise organizations' need for stability and reliability. Conversely, there's Eclipse MicroProfile, with fast interactions and constant innovation. In parallel, the Jakarta EE platform keeps evolving and adopting comprehensive MicroProfile technologies. All this is happening as you read, so it's time to finally comprehend what's happening in the open community and what to expect from a data solution perspective.

Java engineers seeking to deliver scalable enterprise solutions that smoothly enable distributed architectures mostly rely on a platform that can support cloud-native and traditional solutions. In the corporate world, given the long-term adoption of Java, there's a frequent requirement for flexible technologies that can bring the best out of existing technologies and infrastructure without giving up on the opportunity of delivering new cloud-native solutions. In this context, the Jakarta EE platform is a great choice.

The specification of Jakarta EE is huge and impacts the whole Java community; it is essential to highlight that if you're using Spring, Micronaut, or Quarkus, you're using Jakarta EE even indirectly. In this chapter, we'll check the specifications that Jakarta EE covers.

We'll cover the following topics in this chapter:

- Jakarta EE overview
- Framework unveiled—reflection versus reflectionless solutions
- **Java Persistence API (JPA)** state of affairs
- The power of JPA with Quarkus and Panache cloud-native runtimes
- General JPA-related performance considerations

Technical requirements

For this chapter, you will need the following:

- Java 17
- Git
- Maven
- Any preferred IDE

The code for this chapter can be found in the following GitHub repository:

```
https://github.com/PacktPublishing/Persistence-Best-Practices-for-
Java-Applications/tree/main/chapter-05
```

Jakarta EE overview

At the heart of Jakarta EE lies its collection of specifications, each addressing specific aspects of enterprise architecture. These specifications, commonly called the "EE specifications," are designed to cover various use cases encountered in enterprise application development. They provide standardized approaches and guidelines for implementing key functionalities, ensuring interoperability and portability across different implementations.

The Jakarta EE specifications cater to a broad spectrum of enterprise architecture needs, including the following:

- **Web applications**: The Jakarta Servlet specification provides a platform-independent API for building web applications. It defines how web requests and responses are handled, allowing developers to create dynamic, interactive, secure web-based solutions.

- **Enterprise integration**: The **Jakarta Messaging** (**JMS**) specification provides a messaging system enabling seamless communication between distributed application components. It ensures a reliable and asynchronous exchange of information, facilitating integration across disparate systems.

- **Persistence**: The JPA specification simplifies database access and manipulation by providing an **object-relational mapping (ORM)** framework. It allows developers to interact with relational databases using Java objects, abstracting the underlying SQL operations. We can include the Jakarta Bean Validation specification to define constraints on Java driven by annotations; further more, new specifications are coming to support NoSQL and **domain-driven design (DDD)** repositories.

- **Dependency injection (DI)**: The Jakarta **Contexts Dependency Injection (CDI)** specification facilitates loose coupling and promotes modular development by managing object creation, wiring, and life cycle management. It enables the easy integration of different components within an application, enhancing maintainability and testability.

- **Security**: The Jakarta Security specification offers a comprehensive set of APIs and services for securing enterprise applications. It provides authentication, authorization, and data protection mechanisms, helping developers build secure applications and protect sensitive information.

- **RESTful web services**: The **Jakarta RESTful Web Services (JAX-RS)** specification simplifies the development of web services using the **Representational State Transfer (REST)** architectural style. It provides a set of annotations and APIs for building scalable, lightweight, and interoperable web APIs.

The following diagram shows an overview of Jakarta EE 10 API, where you see the huge number of specifications that can help you as a software engineer; another area of the diagram is related to profiles. Currently, there are three profiles that you can use based on your needs:

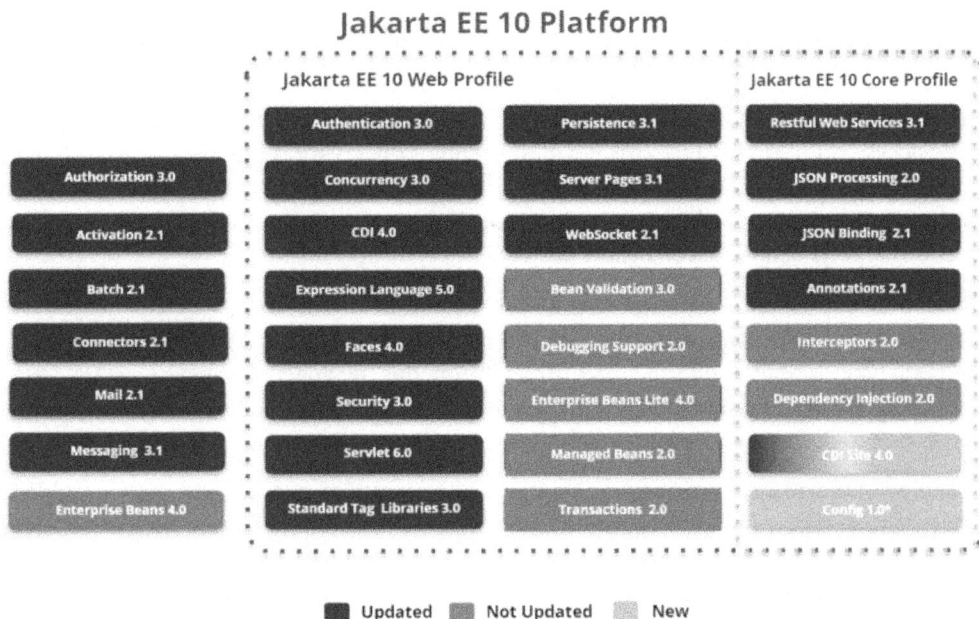

Figure 5.1 – Jakarta EE 10 specification

These are just a few examples of the extensive specifications available in Jakarta EE. Each specification addresses specific requirements, ensuring developers have the tools and guidelines to tackle various enterprise architecture challenges.

By adhering to Jakarta EE specifications, developers can create portable applications across different application servers and vendors, allowing flexibility and scalability. The specifications foster interoperability and compatibility, enabling seamless integration with other systems and services.

Those specifications will help you with modern concepts, approaches, and architectural models. In the Jakarta EE 10 API, we have the CDI Lite specification, where the goal is to reduce reflection, but what is wrong with reflection? In the next section, let's talk about this in more detail.

Framework unveiled – reflection versus reflectionless solutions

Java frameworks are crucial in simplifying and accelerating application development by providing reusable components, predefined structures, and standard methodologies. These frameworks encapsulate common functionalities and design patterns, allowing developers to focus on business logic rather than low-level implementation details.

One fundamental concept in Java programming and many Java frameworks is reflection. Reflection enables a program to examine and modify its structure and behavior at runtime dynamically. It provides a mechanism for inspecting and manipulating classes, interfaces, methods, and fields, even if they are unknown at compile time.

Reflection is essential to developers for several reasons. Here, we list some of these:

- **Dynamic code execution**: Reflection allows developers to instantiate classes, invoke methods, and access fields at runtime. This flexibility enables the creation of flexible, extensible, and customizable applications. For example, frameworks such as Spring and Hibernate heavily rely on reflection to dynamically create and wire dependencies, perform data mapping, and handle various aspects of application behavior.

- **Metadata extraction**: Reflection enables the extraction of metadata associated with classes, methods, and fields. This metadata may include information such as annotations, modifiers, generic types, and method signatures. By analyzing this metadata, developers can implement advanced application functionalities and behavior. For instance, frameworks such as JUnit use reflection to discover and execute test cases based on annotations.

- **Frameworks and annotations**: Java frameworks often utilize annotations, markers added to classes, methods, or fields to provide additional information or configure specific behaviors. Frameworks such as Spring, JPA, and Java Servlet extensively use annotations and reflection to simplify configuration and customization. Reflection allows frameworks to scan and process these annotations at runtime, enabling automatic configuration, DI, and **Aspect-Oriented Programming (AOP)**.

However, while reflection offers excellent flexibility and power, it can impact the performance of Java applications during startup. The process of introspecting classes and loading metadata dynamically can introduce significant overhead, especially in serverless or cloud-native environments where fast startup times are crucial.

> **Why does this matter? Native compilation for Java applications**
>
> A great example is the creation of natively executable Java applications, where developers use **Java virtual machines** (**JVMs**) such as GraalVM (Oracle) and Mandrel (Red Hat) to compile these applications and generate native binaries. This process, based on **ahead-of-time** (**AOT**) compilation, results in the inability to use some behaviors during runtime—including reflection. The AOT compiler does static code analysis during build time to create a native executable, which means that all processing done via dynamic loading (such as reflection, the **Java Native Interface** (**JNI**), or proxies) represents potential issues for this use case.

To address this issue, frameworks such as Quarkus and Micronaut have adopted an alternative approach known as the **build-time** or **compile-time** approach. Instead of relying on *runtime* reflection, these frameworks leverage annotations to capture necessary metadata *during the build process*. Doing so eliminates costly reflection operations at runtime and delivers faster startup times and improved performance.

The next diagram illustrates how both approaches work, where with reflection Java reads the annotations and any metadata in real time, generating more flexibility and pluggability on reading time; this demands more memory and warmup time. We can read this information at the build time, where we get a better warmup and save more memory at the start; however, we lose our flexibility with reflection. As usual, this is a point of trade-off analysis:

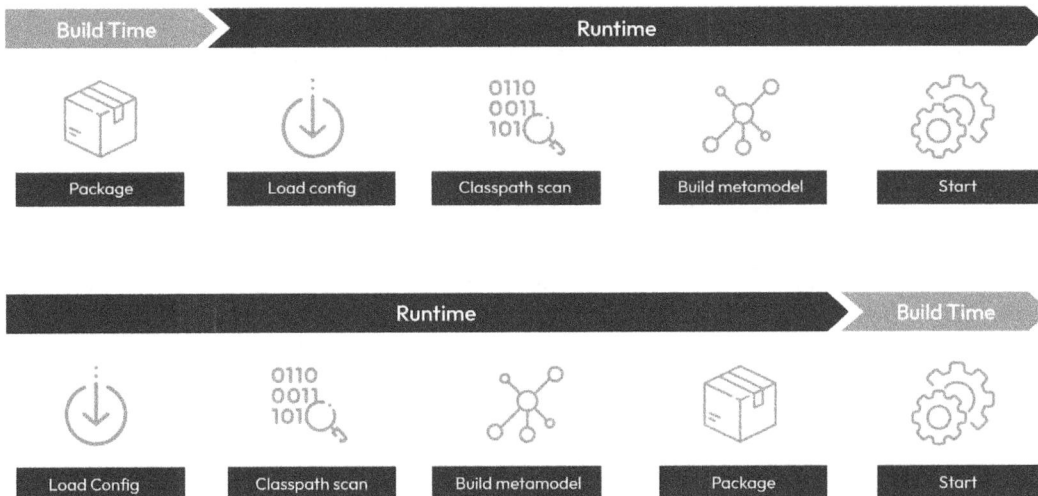

Build Time	Runtime			
Package	Load config	Classpath scan	Build metamodel	Start

Runtime				Build Time
Load Config	Classpath scan	Build metamodel	Package	Start

Figure 5.2 – Reading Java annotations at runtime versus build time

Reflection is a powerful mechanism in Java programming and frameworks. It enables dynamic code execution, metadata extraction, and the utilization of annotations for configuration and customization. While reflection can impact startup performance in specific scenarios, frameworks such as Quarkus and Micronaut have introduced build-time reflection as a solution, allowing developers to leverage the benefits of annotations without sacrificing performance. This approach, enabled by CDI Lite, promotes efficient usage of Java in serverless and cloud-native environments.

Jakarta EE platform constant evolution – CDI Lite

Based on the needs and impacts highlighted so far, the Jakarta EE platform released as version 10 has changes to the CDI specification that accommodate many behaviors helpful for this scenario. The CDI Lite specification brings behaviors needed by these frameworks and aims to provide a lightweight version of CDI. CDI Lite leverages *compile-time reflection* to eliminate the runtime overhead associated with full CDI implementations, making it suitable for resource-constrained environments and serverless architectures.

Developers can choose between frameworks that employ reflection or follow a reflectionless approach when developing Java applications. This comparison table will explore critical aspects such as annotation reading, warmup flexibility, and encapsulation in these two Java frameworks. Understanding the trade-offs and advantages of each approach can help developers make informed decisions based on their project requirements and development preferences.

	Reflection	**Reflectionless**
Read Java annotations	Real-time	Build time
Warmup (extra time required by the framework on startup)	It has a slow startup	It has a faster startup
Flexibility	Pluggability in real time	Limitation by build time
Encapsulation	Strong encapsulation	More limitations at the Java encapsulation

Table 5.1 – Reflection versus reflectionless solution

When we talk about the application, we're not sure about the architecture style, such as microservices or monolith, or whether we'll use a real-time or build-time Java application; however, for the majority of the solutions, we'll use any persistence engine. Let's now discuss in more detail the most mature Jakarta persistence specification: JPA.

JPA state of affairs

JPA is a crucial Jakarta EE specification and the most mature data specification for enterprise applications. It provides a standardized and robust approach to ORM in Java, enabling developers to interact seamlessly with relational databases.

When working with the integration between Java applications and relational databases, several aspects need to be taken into consideration, such as the following:

- **Configuration management**: How the configurations are externalized in order to be easily yet securely changed based on the environment in which it is being deployed (dev, prod, and so on).

- **Connection handling**: Improper handling of connections with the database may lead to extra processing time, as it is expensive. This need is related to the requirement of managing open, close, and track connections with the database in order to use resources effectively and avoid having too many open and idle connections or not enough connections available to the application.

- **Mapping classes to database tables**: As we saw in previous chapters, mapping objects may be implemented in multiple ways and provide a higher or lower level of flexibility and abstraction.

- **Mapping the relation between classes**: OOP brings concepts such as hierarchy, which is not available in a relational database schema. Depending on the way these classes are configured, data management can have higher complexity and maintenance costs.

- **Transaction management**: Managing transactions and assuring atomicity and rollbacks at the application layer.

- **Code generation**: Developers can either write pure SQL queries or rely on abstractions to speed up the development time. Currently, some frameworks can abstract most basic CRUD queries. Unfortunately, if misused, code generation may lead to slow queries and restrictions on the proper usage of private methods.

- **Fetching strategies**: Allows the retrieval of data in ways to take the best advantage of memory consumption, and when properly used, brings performance improvements as data will only be fetched from the database when needed. This is related to the well-known lazy/eager fetching modes available, for example, on Hibernate.

- **Decoupling business logic from technical aspects**: Based on their goals, a developer can create extremely flexible and customized code (for example, using JDBC) in exchange for negatively impacting code coupling between the data persistence layer and the business logic layer.

Considering these recurrent needs of Java developers and the possibility to create reproducible good practices that could be easily and largely adopted, the JPA specification has evolved since its creation.

The following diagram shows the ecosystem of JPA as the most mature persistence specification in the Jakarta EE world; several vendors and frameworks use it, and we can also apply several persistence patterns such as Active Record, Repository, and Mapper:

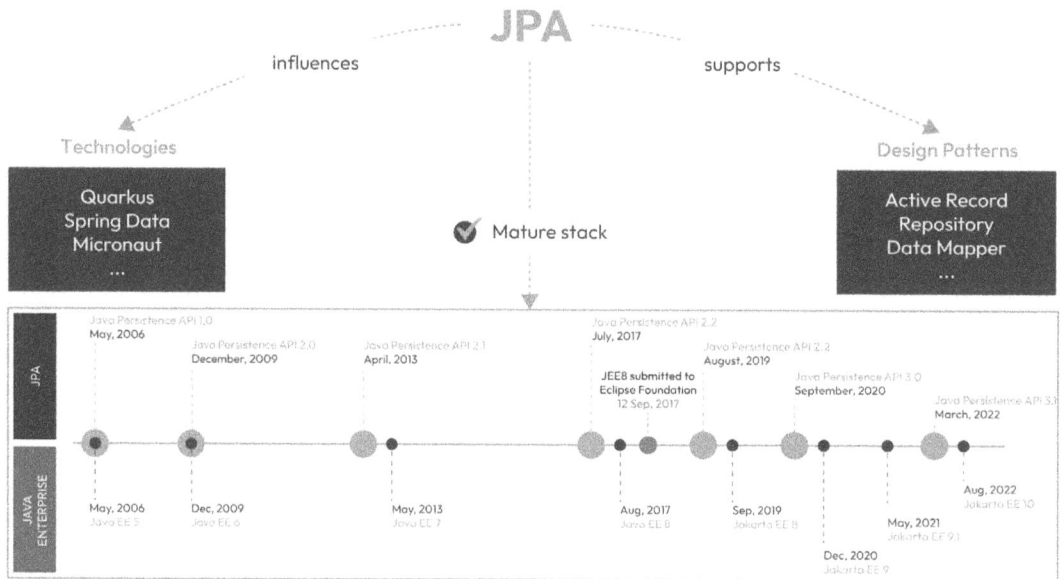

Figure 5.3 – JPA timeline and landscape

When combined with frameworks such as Spring and Quarkus, JPA offers the flexibility to implement different design approaches, including Active Record, Mapper, and Repository patterns. Let's delve into these design approaches and explore how JPA can operate by reading annotations using reflection or at build time.

JPA and database mapping patterns

When working with JPA, developers mostly adopt three design options: Active Record, Mapper, and Repository. Notice that due to JPA capabilities such as mapping entities and their relationships to each other, abstractions for basic database operations, and exception-handling mechanisms, adopting the patterns becomes simpler. Let's take a closer look at this:

- **Active Record with JPA**: In this approach, the domain model class encapsulates the persistence logic, following the Active Record pattern. It simplifies database operations as the domain classes are active participants and are responsible for handling CRUD operations and relationships directly.

    When relying on JPA, it is possible to annotate a domain class with JPA annotations such as @Entity to mark it as a persistent entity. The domain class can also be annotated with @Table, which will define which is the corresponding database table that should be mapped to this entity. These annotations' metadata enables JPA to map the object attributes to the respective database columns.

- **Mapper**: According to the Mapper pattern, the domain model and the persistence logic should be separated with the help of new and dedicated mapper classes.

  JPA, in combination with frameworks such as Spring and Quarkus, allows developers to configure and manage these mappers. The mappers handle the conversion between the domain objects and the database tables, abstracting the persistence details from the domain model. JPA's `EntityManager` and `EntityManagerFactory` classes provide the necessary APIs to perform database operations, while the mapper classes facilitate the mapping between the database and the domain model.

- **Repositories**: The Repository pattern suggests introducing a layer of abstraction between the application domain layers and the data access layer.

  When developing with JPA, developers can define repository interfaces that act as contracts specifying the available CRUD operations and queries. JPA's `EntityManager` class is the underlying mechanism for executing queries and managing transactions, enabling efficient and scalable data access.

  Frameworks such as Spring Data JPA and Quarkus support repositories and can automatically generate the necessary implementation code based on the defined interfaces.

When considering the usage of frameworks to implement patterns, we should be aware of the pros and cons. We will delve into a detailed code example, but before that, let's check the items to be aware of.

Based on the application use case and requirements, it would be recommended to know what happens under the covers and what limitations your application will inherit from the framework you are choosing. When using Active Record with Panache and Quarkus, for instance, your entity might be extending the `PanacheEntity` class. With Repository, it might be extending `JpaRepository`, a generic Spring Data JPA interface. By knowing the chosen framework implementation details, you can better identify where you are opting to tightly couple your application code with the framework, by using exclusive annotations or dependencies. You'd be aware whether and if so, to what extent there will be a violation of the principle of **separation of concerns** (**SoC**), or for instance, the extra effort that will be needed in case of the need of migration to a different persistence framework.

The pros and cons we learned about in *Chapter 4* apply here as well: Active Record will be less complex than Repository, whereas adopting Repository can result in better SoC than Active Record, resulting in enhanced maintainability and testability.

We'll delve into a comprehensive code sample to clarify the trade-offs between choosing the convenience offered by frameworks versus adhering to well-known coding best practices.

The power of JPA with Quarkus and Panache cloud-native runtimes

To demonstrate how modern persistence frameworks enable developers to rely on their knowledge of JPA, let's take a look at Quarkus and Panache, and the experience of developing cloud-native Java services with accelerated development speed. Within this context, we'll evaluate key aspects of design pattern implementation, automatically generated persistence code, and some potential drawbacks to take into consideration when designing a solution.

You can either follow along or create a brand-new project to try the following code. If you haven't used Quarkus and Panache yet, you may notice quite a difference in the development experience of a lightweight runtime compared to traditional application servers, and the simplicity of coding straightforward CRUD scenarios with Panache.

Details on how to create the project can be found in the project's repository: `https://github.com/architects4j/mastering-java-persistence-book-samples/edit/main/chapter-05/README.md`. Now, let's dive into it.

The microservice we're about to see will be used to manage *books* and *magazines*, and we'll explore two different database design patterns using JPA: Repository and Active Record.

Setting up the new service

As we will rely on features for persistence and REST endpoints (easily generated through the Quarkus starter page), the project needs dependencies to handle such capabilities. Interestingly, much of the hard work will be automatically generated by the frameworks, which in turn, are actually based on well-known specifications and technologies such as RESTEasy, JSON-B, Hibernate ORM, Hibernate Validator, Panache, and JDBC.

The underlying storage will be handled by H2, an in-memory data storage, which should be useful for learning purposes as it doesn't require installation of external databases or usage of Docker to bootstrap one database instance. However, remember that H2 is not recommended for production usage.

The first difference shows up in the Quarkus project's configuration (`src/main/resources/application.properties`), as developers can rely on a single properties configuration file to have h2 as the database kind and `memory` as the JDBC URL. This approach enables changes to the underlying database technology without any code modification (for example, from H2 to PostgreSQL, MariaDB, or others).

Another positive aspect is that this configuration style relies on the Eclipse MicroProfile Configuration specification, which has out-of-the-box support for overwriting the application's properties based on the environment in which the application is running—in other words, this is how sensible data (such as the username and password) within production environments can remain confidential and not be configured directly at the application level.

The property configuration could be set up as follows:

```
quarkus.datasource.db-kind=h2
quarkus.datasource.username=username-default
quarkus.datasource.jdbc.url=jdbc:h2:mem:default
quarkus.datasource.jdbc.max-size=13
quarkus.hibernate-
   orm.dialect=org.hibernate.dialect.H2Dialect
quarkus.hibernate-orm.database.generation=create
quarkus.hibernate-orm.log.sql=true
```

Persistent entities and database operations

With the foundation ready to go, the project's entities are created next. We'll start by checking the two patterns from this moment forward, where you can observe the Book entity is implemented using Active Record, and Magazine using the Repository pattern.

The Book class is represented as follows. Note that even though it brings the @Entity annotation, there are no additional attribute-level annotations. Also, the Book entity "knows" its database operations, including, for instance, how to search for books by name and book release:

```
@Entity
public class Book extends PanacheEntity {
    public String name;
    public int release;
    public int edition;

    public static List<Book> findByName(String name) {
        return list("name", name);
    }

    public static List<Book> findByRelease(int year) {
        return list("release", year);
    }
}
```

As you'll see next, the Magazine class uses classic JPA annotations such as @Entity and @id (so far, nothing new under the sun). The reason why the Book entity does not require an @id annotation is that it inherits such capability from the class it extends, PanacheEntity. PanacheEntity handles several operations, through heritage, including the id attribute:

```
@Entity
public class Magazine {
    @Id
```

```
    @GeneratedValue
    public Long id;
    public String name;
    public int release;
    public int edition;
}
```

Differently from the class being implemented with Active Record where the database operation will be at the entity itself, the `Magazine` class requires an additional class to do such data manipulation—a `Repository` class. The `MagazineRepository` class has to implement the essential database procedures, plus the queries (such as `find by release and name`, as available in the `Book` class). As we are using the `PanacheRepository` class, we can save some time on the basic operations as they will be automatically generated by Panache later on.

The `MagazineRepository` code is presented here:

```
@ApplicationScoped
public class MagazineRepository implements
  PanacheRepository<Magazine> {
    public List<Magazine> findByName(String name) {
        return list("name", name);
    }

    public List<Magazine> findByRelease(int year) {
        return list("release", year);
    }
}
```

Exposing REST endpoints for data manipulation

Finally, to manipulate data through the classes we've checked so far, the application exposes REST APIs. The endpoints are `BookResource` and `MagazineResource`, which should expose the same database operations for `Book` and `Magazine` so that we can evaluate the differences in the usage of each approach. The first difference that can be mentioned is that, while we don't need to inject anything in order to use the `BookResource` endpoint, to manipulate the `Magazine` entity, the developer must inject the respective `repository` class.

First, observe how the `BookResource` endpoint allows interactions with `Book`, the entity implemented with Active Record. You'll notice as a negative aspect the fact that there is a tighter coupling between the endpoint and the Active Record. As a positive point, notice how it allows the app to be simpler, with fewer layers.

The BookResource class includes the following:

- Three GET endpoints: findAll, findByName, and findByYear

- One POST and one DELETE method

The code is shown here:

```
@Path("/library")
@Consumes(MediaType.APPLICATION_JSON)
@Produces(MediaType.APPLICATION_JSON)
public class BookResource {

    @GET
    public List<Book> findAll() {
        return Book.listAll();
    }

    @GET
    @Path("name/{name}")
    public List<Book> findByName(@PathParam("name") String
      name) {
        return Book.findByName(name);
    }

    @GET
    @Path("release/{year}")
    public List<Book> findByYear(@PathParam("year") int
      year) {
        return Book.findByRelease(year);
    }

    @POST
@Transactional
    public Book insert(Book book) {
        book.persist();
        return book;
    }

    @DELETE
    @Path("{id}")
    @Transactional
    public void delete(@PathParam("id") Long id) {
        Book.deleteById(id);
    }
}
```

In the preceding code, observe that the `Book` entity already offers the methods that execute operations against the database.

Now, let's move on to the `MagazineResource` endpoint, which covers the Repository pattern. Observe that even though this is a simple example project, it will increase the complexity of the business requirements and time with the erosion of architecture in real life. It reminds us of *Chapter 4*, where we covered more about the layers and their trade-offs, so the same layer that can help us, in isolation, break what into pieces might impact more complex code. As the application expands and incorporates additional layers such as the service layer, or as it adopts a hexagonal model, it becomes crucial to carefully analyze the trade-offs and pay close attention to the design of persistence layers.

Here is the implementation of the `MagazineResource` endpoint:

```java
@Path("/magazines")
@Consumes(MediaType.APPLICATION_JSON)
@Produces(MediaType.APPLICATION_JSON)
public class MagazineResource {

    @Inject
    MagazineRepository repository;

    @GET
    public List<Magazine> findAll() {
        return repository.listAll();
    }

    @GET
    @Path("name/{name}")
    public List<Magazine> findByName(@PathParam("name")
      String name) {
        return repository.findByName(name);
    }

    @GET
    @Path("release/{year}")
    public List<Magazine> findByYear(@PathParam("year") int
      year) {
        return repository.findByRelease(year);
    }

    @POST
    @Transactional
    public Magazine insert(Magazine magazine) {
        this.repository.persist(magazine);
```

```
        return magazine;
    }

    @DELETE
    @Path("{id}")
    @Transactional
    public void delete(@PathParam("id") Long id) {
        repository.deleteById(id);
    }
}
```

Key points to observe in the preceding class are set out here:

- The developer is required to inject an instance of the `MagazineRepository` endpoint
- The developer must implement the class and the methods that are needed, obtaining a greater level of control and customization of the underlying implementation, plus code with better SoC between the domain entity and the database integration

At this point, the application is ready, and all operations are ready to be accessed via REST and by correctly manipulating data through the methods defined by the developer and provided out of the box by Panache.

Even faster development speed – automatic endpoint generation

Panache allows even more development speed for standard scenarios, combining the benefits of Active Record we've seen with the automatic generation of REST endpoints. The following capabilities are offered by the `quarkus-hibernate-orm-rest-data-panache` Quarkus extension, instead of the previously used `quarkus-hibernate-orm-panache` extension.

The speed at which a developer can deliver a completely usable CRUD service is extremely noticeable when compared to the previous approach, and even more so if compared to traditional EE application servers. With the following steps, a developer should be able to create a whole CRUD for *newsletters* in just a few minutes.

Taking into consideration the existing project, a new `Newsletter` class could be created as follows:

```
@Entity
public class Newsletter extends PanacheEntity {
    public String author;
    public String headline;
}
```

It relies on the Active Record implementation as well. On top of that, it combines Quarkus and Panache capabilities for automatically generating REST endpoints based on Panache entities.

To achieve the same results as the examples covered before, the following REST operations should be available:

- Three GET resources: `findAll`, `findById`, and `getCount`
- POST, PUT, and DELETE, to enable inserting, updating, and deleting newsletters, respectively

To achieve this objective, all that is needed is a new interface that extends the `PanacheEntityResource` interface. The interface indicates the Panache entity that is the `id` attribute type:

```
import io.quarkus.hibernate.orm.rest.data.panache.
PanacheEntityResource;
public interface NewsletterResource extends
PanacheEntityResource<Newsletter, Long> {
}
```

And that's all! If running Quarkus using dev mode, the developer should already be able to validate the results simply by refreshing the page and checking the `swagger-ui` page and the new endpoints, as shown here:

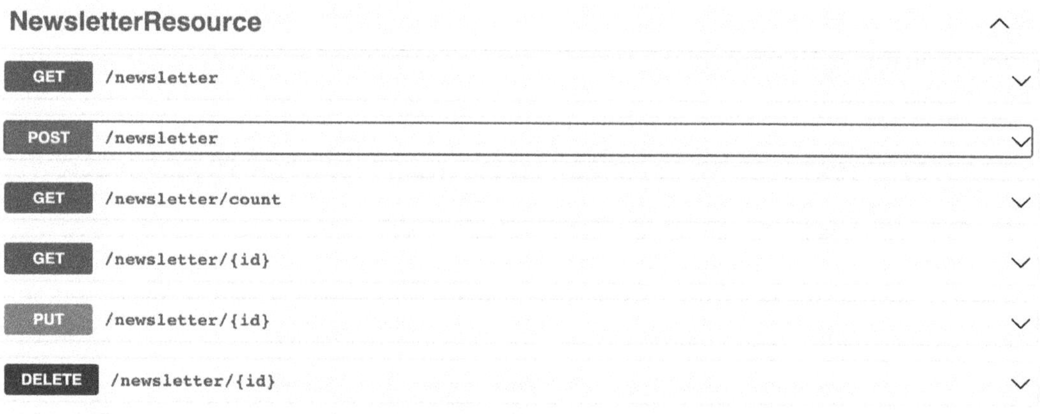

NewsletterResource

GET	/newsletter
POST	/newsletter
GET	/newsletter/count
GET	/newsletter/{id}
PUT	/newsletter/{id}
DELETE	/newsletter/{id}

Figure 5.4 – New endpoints automatically generated by Panache

Now, be aware that when choosing to go down this route, all the attributes are configured as public attributes. And here's your trade-off when using such an approach: unless you add extra code to be able to handle the usage of private attributes, you will opt for development speed in exchange for completely giving up on encapsulation, no access control, increased code coupling (as changes to the class may result in potential changes to other classes), and limited control and data integrity (the attribute can be directly modified).

You may think it is as simple as configuring the attributes as private and adding public getters and setters. True—this is mostly the same. But you would lack encapsulation in the very same way (as the setter is still public) with "dumb" getters and setters. Plus, that is exactly what Panache (in the current version at the time of writing) does under the covers: it generates `getter` and `setter` attributes and rewrites every usage of these attributes to the respective `getter` and `setter` attribute.

Panache is very powerful and allows developers to also be more efficient when writing queries, where it would be possible—for example—to use code such as `Newsletter.find("order by author")`, or `Newletter.find("author = ?1 and headline = ?2", "karina", "Java lives!")`, or, even better, `Newsletter.find("author", "karina")`.

You have seen the amazing experience Java developers can get from modern runtime technologies and how effective it can be to create from scratch a completely new stateful service while relying on existing knowledge of JPA. Next, we'll slightly shift to another topic, highlighting considerations on concerns commonly faced by most developers and architects who have ever worked with JPA: performance and scalability.

General JPA-related performance considerations

The following considerations apply not only to Panache but also to JPA-based applications in general. To help identify or go through the performance tuning process, you can always rely on the framework capabilities of outputting the DDLs being executed (database SQL operations) and the database operations statistics. Hibernate, for example, offers several configuration parameters such as `show_sql`, `generate_statistics`, `jdbc.batch_size`, `default_batch_fetch_size`, and `cache.use_query_cache`. In the following paragraphs, you'll find considerations revolving around such configurations. For now, check here how some configuration could be applied to the sample Quarkus application example we just created. These properties allow the logging of DDLs and statistics:

```
quarkus.hibernate-orm.log.sql=true
quarkus.hibernate-orm.statistics=true
quarkus.hibernate-orm.metrics.enabled=true
quarkus.log.level=DEBUG
```

Note that verbose logging configuration should not be used in production as it directly impacts application performance; plus, the application log categories can be configured individually to output only what you need. As an example, the preceding statistics configuration can help you identify slow execution DDLs. See one example of information you can obtain for each database operation:

```
2023-06-19 02:10:25,402 DEBUG [org.hib.sta.int.StatisticsImpl]
(executor-thread-1) HHH000117: HQL: SELECT COUNT(*) FROM dev.a4j.
mastering.data.Newsletter, time: 1ms, rows: 1
```

If you are worried about performance, certify your code (either due to mapping or query parsing) is not *automatically generating slow-performing SQL queries* under the covers, *fetching unnecessary information* when not needed, or *automatically generating too many queries* instead of running a better-suited single one.

Other than the persistence-related Java code itself, it is also possible to fine-tune your JPA data source connection by setting the number of connections to be opened by the application during startup, the connection pool size (so that open connections can be reused), and how you want the application (via your framework and class of choice) to identify and clean idle or unclosed connections.

Another item to consider is batch operations. Let's say each newsletter can contain several articles, and an author can create a new newsletter along with 50 articles, all at once. In this case, instead of going back and forth between the application and the database 51 times to create all articles and the newsletter, it would be possible to do it only once to execute all operations. The same applies to querying data.

For applications with an intensive number of queries, focus on creating specific SQL queries that can perform better, and if the app requires several query executions, it is recommended to fine-tune the batch-and-fetch size on the application configuration. JDBC batch operations are a good approach to defining how many operations can be executed in a single database roundtrip.

For applications with an intensive number of inserts, it is also possible to use bulk inserts, making sure to avoid long-running transactions or spending extra time each time the "flush" operation occurs (as `EntityManager` will have to handle the insert of a large set of objects at once). As applied to most fine-tuning configurations, the best way to evaluate which would be the best configuration to set on each application is to execute load tests and compare results. Still ,in the context of querying data, remember that caching frequently used queries helps reduce the number of database hits and improves performance.

In regard to caching in the JPA context, there are two types of cache: first- and second-level cache. The first-level cache relates to the objects contained within the `EntityManager` cache (session cache). It allows the app to save time when accessing objects that were recently accessed or manipulated within a session.

When working with distributed applications scaled up to many running instances, it may be beneficial to consider a second-level cache that allows the usage of a shared cache. Remember that caching features are not recommended for 100% of scenarios, because even though it may lead to significantly better performance, it will demand a good understanding of how to fine-tune the caching solution.

Finally, fine-tuning a cache solution means providing proper cache invalidation (to make sure the cache data is aligned with the underlying database's current data), proper cache synchronization (as there may be multiple cache provider instances), eviction policies, and more. In scenarios where there is real-time or up-to-date data, take into consideration the challenges of cache usage and the introduced possibility of data staleness.

This brings us to the end of our Quarkus and JPA journey, where we have seen both Active Record and Repository patterns with JPA. We can see how easy Active Record can be, but at the same time, my entity knows and executes database operations. Thus, it has two responsibilities. This is fine when we talk about a redirect or any integral functions that do not require a huge demand of business complexity.

Summary

In conclusion, Jakarta EE is a robust platform that provides a comprehensive set of specifications, APIs, and tools for developing enterprise applications. Within the persistence layer, Jakarta EE shines with its mature JPA specification, which offers a standardized approach to ORM. With JPA, developers can leverage design patterns such as Active Record and Repository to simplify and streamline their data access operations.

When combined with the Quarkus framework, JPA in Jakarta EE demonstrates its capabilities in practice. Quarkus, known for its fast startup time and efficient resource utilization, enhances the development experience by seamlessly integrating with JPA. Developers can leverage the Active Record pattern, allowing their domain model classes to handle persistence operations directly. Alternatively, they can adopt the Repository pattern, which introduces an abstraction layer for flexible and scalable data access. By leveraging JPA within Quarkus, developers can efficiently interact with relational databases, ensure data integrity, and achieve optimal performance in their Jakarta EE applications.

Overall, with its mature JPA specification, Jakarta EE, in conjunction with the Quarkus framework, empowers developers to build robust and efficient persistence layers. The combination of Jakarta EE's standardized approach to persistence and Quarkus' streamlined development experience opens up a world of possibilities for creating scalable and high-performing enterprise applications. But how about NoSQL? Does Jakarta EE have support for it? Yes, it does; the following chapter will cover how to handle several NoSQL database types such as key-value, document, and graph with Java.

6

NoSQL in Java Demystified – One API to Rule Them All

NoSQL databases have gained significant popularity recently, and this chapter explores why they deserve more attention. With the evolution of software and increased diverse requirements, NoSQL databases offer an easier route to success. Using the Jakarta standard, this persistence type is helpful in various areas, including more traditional sectors such as finance. NoSQL databases provide flexible data modeling, horizontal scaling, and better performance, among other advantages. As a result, they are suitable for managing large amounts of structured or unstructured data and have become a popular choice for modern applications. This chapter will guide us on how to use NoSQL databases with Java, helping developers exploit their features and capabilities.

We will cover the following topics in this chapter:

- Understanding NoSQL database trade-offs
- Consuming NoSQL databases with **Jakarta NoSQL (JNoSQL)**
- Graph databases

Technical requirements

The following are required for this chapter

- Java 17
- Git
- Maven
- Docker
- Any preferred IDE

- The code for this chapter can be found at `https://github.com/PacktPublishing/Persistence-Best-Practices-for-Java-Applications/tree/main/chapter-06`.

Understanding NoSQL database trade-offs

NoSQL databases are popular, including several persistence solutions offered by the top database engines. It is essential to remember that NoSQL databases do not eliminate the need for relational databases.

SQL databases remain crucial to most enterprise solutions. They are where people more often start to learn to program, and there are numerous articles and books written on the topic.

Furthermore, the maturity of the products that use SQL is vast! Those products can help you with crucial tasks, such as backups, migrations, and query analysis.

The goal is not to demotivate you from using NoSQL. However, once you are a senior engineer, remember the second law of software architecture mentioned in *Fundamentals of Software Architecture: An Engineering Approach* by Neal Ford: everything has a trade-off!

Consider that, and let's move on to the NoSQL database.

Consuming NoSQL databases with JNoSQL

We are lucky to have several solutions and success cases in the Java platform. Thus, the next step is to create a standard API as soon as this technology matures.

The JNoSQL specification aims to simplify the communication between Java and NoSQL databases.

The benefit of standardizing the behavior and interface of multiple NoSQL databases is code portability and ease of integration. We usually talk about switching the database, which is true. However, the most significant advantage is to make it easier for everybody to work on a project. When it is required, you can switch databases naturally.

ArangoDB

```
BaseDocument baseDocument = new BaseDocument();
baseDocument.addAttribute(name, value);
```

mongoDB

```
Document document = new Document();
document.append(name, value);
```

Couchbase

```
JsonObject jsonObject = JsonObject.create();
jsonObject.put(name, value);
```

OrientDB

```
ODocument document = new ODocument("collection");
document.field(name, value);
```

Figure 6.1: NoSQL databases – document type

There are great benefits to using a standard API; furthermore, you can use particular behavior, such as **Cassandra Query Language (CQL)** for Cassandra and **ArangoDB Query Language (AQL)** for ArangoDB.

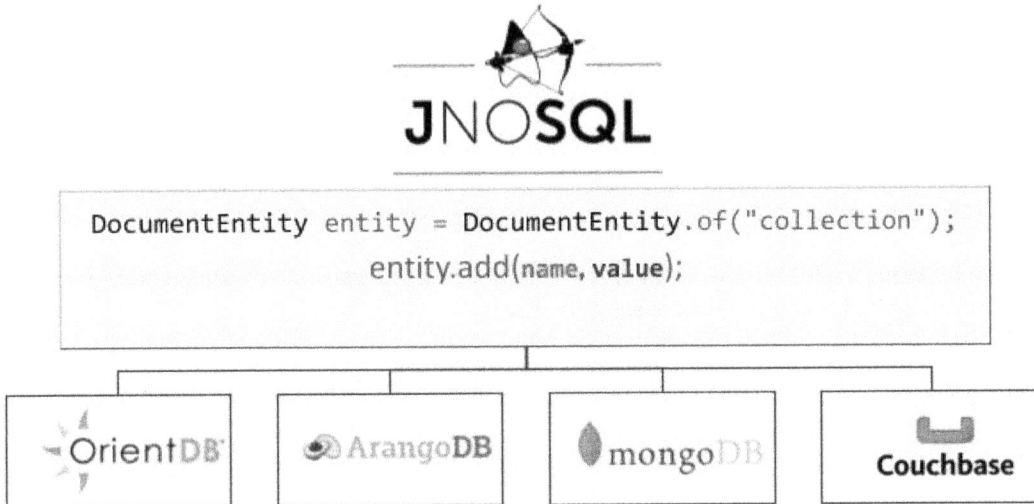

Figure 6.2: NoSQL databases – document type with a single API

This is the main principle of JNoSQL, to simplify and make your and your organization's life easier when it comes to Java and NoSQL databases. On the spec side, you can explore your entities; for example, with JPA, you can use annotations to operate with several NoSQL database types, such as document, column, graph, and key-value. See how the same annotations work in several document databases:

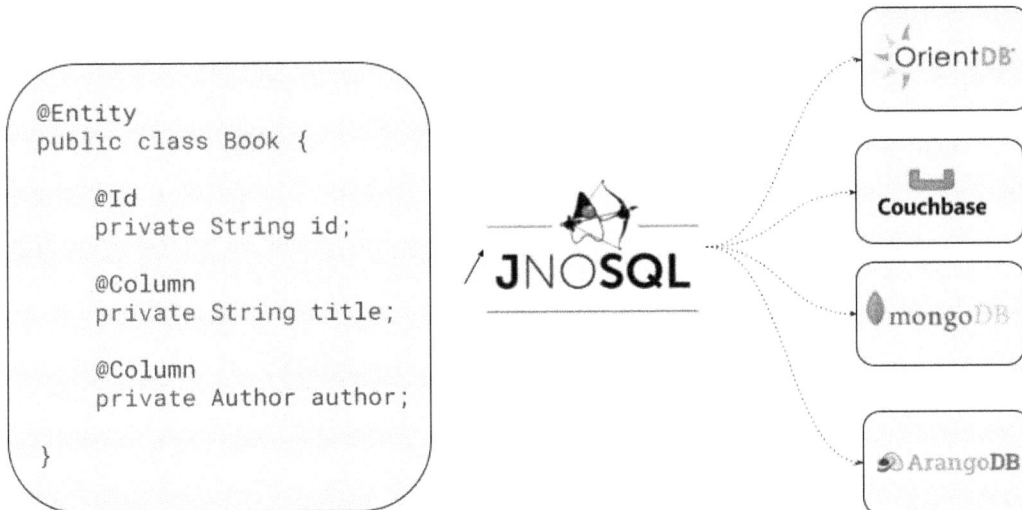

Figure 6.3: JNoSQL abstraction for multiple database integrations

The spec supports the most popular NoSQL types: key-value, document, wide-column or other column types, and graph.

Key-value databases

Starting with the simplest one: key-value. This NoSQL solution flavor has a structure that looks like a map. Thus, you can generally find information from the key, and the value is a blob. Each vendor has a different way of serializing and storing the value, such as text, JSON, or binary JSON.

Using the library system, we can use this database to save the user settings information; thus, we'll create a User entity to preserve the language and categories.

To provide an example of this model, we'll follow a simple Java SE application with JNoSQL. We will use the most popular key-value database solution: Redis.

Defining the configuration of Redis in production would require its own book; we'll install this sample locally, but please, if working in production, check the Redis documentation for more details. For now, once you have Docker configured, run the following command:

```
docker run --name redis-instance -p 6379:6379 -d redis
```

The server is running; the next step is to add dependencies to our project. This sample uses the Maven project, so we'll add the mapping dependency and the Redis driver:

```
<dependency>
    <groupId>org.eclipse.jnosql.mapping</groupId>
    <artifactId>jnosql-mapping-key-value</artifactId>
    <version>${jnosql.version}</version>
</dependency>
<dependency>
    <groupId>org.eclipse.jnosql.communication</groupId>
    <artifactId>jnosql-redis-driver</artifactId>
    <version>${jnosql.version}</version>
</dependency>
```

With the dependencies ready, the next step is to create the User entities with the annotations to map to a key-value database. It requires an annotation to define as a JNoSQL entity and the key, where you'll set the Entity and Id annotations, respectively:

```
@Entity
public class User {

    @Id
    private String userName;
```

```
    private String name;

    private Set<String> languages;

    private Set<String> categories;

  //...
}
```

The Entity and Id annotations are used when defining the User entity class and the userName field, respectively.

Let's execute it. KeyValueTemplate is the instance we use to operate a key-value database; it is the lowest level of mapping communication:

```
public static void main(String[] args) {

    User otavio = User.builder().userName("otaviojava")
            .name("Otavio Santana")
            .category("Technology")
            .category("Philosophy")
            .category("History")
            .language("English")
            .language("Portuguese")
            .language("French").build();

    try (SeContainer container =
      SeContainerInitializer.newInstance().initialize()) {
        KeyValueTemplate template =
          container.select(KeyValueTemplate.class).get();
        User userSaved = template.put(otavio);
        System.out.println("User saved: " + userSaved);
        Optional<User> user = template.get("otaviojava",
          User.class);
        System.out.println("Entity found: " + user);
        template.delete("otaviojava");


    }
}
```

The queries on this database type have limitations, but it is powerful. The **Time To Live** (**TTL**) is a feature used to define the expiration time of the information in a database:

```java
public static void main(String[] args) throws
   InterruptedException {

    User poliana = User.builder()
            .userName("poly")
            .name("Poliana Santana")
            .category("Philosophy")
            .category("History")
            .language("English")
            .language("Portuguese")
            .build();

    try (SeContainer container = SeContainerInitializer
       .newInstance().initialize()) {
        KeyValueTemplate template = container
          .select(KeyValueTemplate.class).get();
        template.put(poliana, Duration.ofSeconds(1));
        System.out.println("The key return: " +
          template.get("poly", User.class));
        TimeUnit.SECONDS.sleep(2L);
        System.out.println("Entity after expired: " +
          template.get("poly", User.class));
        template.delete("poly");

    }
}
```

But wait, where is the configuration? The JNoSQL implementation uses Eclipse MicroProfile configuration to preserve good software practices, such as twelve-factor app.

In this sample, we'll put the properties in the `property` file, but we can overwrite the system environment or include more configurations, such as a username and password:

```
jnosql.keyvalue.database=developers
jnosql.redis.port=6379
jnosql.redis.host=localhost
```

The key-value is a strong ally when you want to save entities that should be fast to read/write. These solutions usually work in memory with a snapshot to avoid data loss if the server goes down.

Like any technology solution, there are trade-offs to consider. For example, while it is possible to retrieve information using an ID and return the value as a unique blob, this approach may not be ideal in all situations. Therefore, let's explore the next type of solution to address this issue.

Column databases

The following database type is the wide-column type, which follows the same principles as key-value, but instead of a unique blob, you can split the information into small columns.

This NoSQL database is also known as a two-dimensional key-value store. The most popular implementation is Apache Cassandra; this section will cover an integration between Java and Apache Cassandra.

As mentioned, we won't cover tips for running in production; for now, we'll run a single instance for test purposes:

```
docker run -d --name cassandra-instance -p 9042:9042 cassandra
```

> **Tip**
> When running a Cassandra instance with Docker, please don't run it this way in production. This configuration is best for your test environment. For production use, go to the Apache Cassandra documentation on the Apache website.

We'll follow the same idea of configuration, so we'll use Java and Maven projects. The first step on the Java side is to add dependencies to the Maven project:

```
<dependency>
    <groupId>org.eclipse.jnosql.mapping</groupId>
    <artifactId>jnosql-cassandra-extension</artifactId>
    <version>${jnosql.version}</version>
</dependency>
```

This dependency seems different because it is a Cassandra extension; it is the column API plus behavior specific to Cassandra, such as CQL. If you wish, you can use it as we did with Redis, but you cannot use Cassandra-specific behavior easily:

```
<dependency>
    <groupId>org.eclipse.jnosql.communication</groupId>
    <artifactId>jnosql-cassandra-driver</artifactId>
    <version>${jnosql.version}</version>
</dependency>
<dependency>
    <groupId>org.eclipse.jnosql.mapping</groupId>
    <artifactId>jnosql-mapping-column</artifactId>
    <version>${project.version}</version>
</dependency>
```

This NoSQL database works differently from SQL. Indeed, denormalization is your best friend.

First, visualize the model. Then, create it. We want to track and view the rental records of a user with a particular ID who rents books:

```java
@Entity("rental")
public class RentalBook {

    @Id("id")
    private UUID id;

    @Column
    private LocalDate date;

    @Column
    @UDT("user")
    private User user;

    @Column
    @UDT("book")
    private Set<Book> books = new HashSet<>();
}
@Entity
public class User {

    @Column
    private String username;

    @Column
    private String name;
}

@Entity
public class Book {

    @Column
    private UUID id;

    @Column
    private String title;
}
```

That's it for the model; from the ID, we can return the track record of a book rental. We're replicating information such as the book's title and the user's name to avoid any joins or more processes, but once a field has been updated, we need to run an event in the background to update it.

The User and Book entities are user-defined types, where we can add multiple values to a single column.

Despite JPA, JNoSQL must define each field to be stored using either a Column or Id annotation.

Let's execute the code, as essentially we can use the same principles and behavior that we did with key-value. We can also select the fields to return in a query instead of always returning everything:

```java
try(SeContainer container =
  SeContainerInitializer.newInstance().initialize()) {

        RentalBook otavio = RentalBook.builder()
                .id(UUID.randomUUID())
                .date(LocalDate.now())
                .user(User.of("otaviojava", "Otavio
                    Santana"))
                .book(Book.of(UUID.randomUUID(), "Clean
                    Code"))
                .book(Book.of(UUID.randomUUID(), "Effective
                    Java"))
                .build();

        RentalBook karina = RentalBook.builder()
                .id(UUID.randomUUID())
                .date(LocalDate.now())
                .user(User.of("kvarel4", "Karina Varela"))
                .book(Book.of(UUID.randomUUID(), "Clean
                Arch"))
                .build();

        ColumnTemplate template =  container
          .select(CassandraTemplate.class).get();

        template.insert(List.of(otavio, karina),
          Duration.ofDays(600L));

        ColumnQuery query = ColumnQuery.select("id",
          "date").from("rental")
                .where("id").eq(karina.getId()).build();

        System.out.println("Executing query using API: ");
        template.select(query).forEach(System.out::println);
```

```
         System.out.println("Executing query using text: ");
         template.query("select * from rental")
           .forEach(System.out::println);


    }
```

Cassandra is not schemaless, although you need to create the schema before using it. Running the query locally is OK, but don't use it in production. This is because it takes time to start and run it in production. The following code shows a configuration for using Cassandra:

```
jnosql.column.database=library
jnosql.cassandra.query.1=CREATE KEYSPACE IF NOT EXISTS library WITH
replication = {'class': 'SimpleStrategy', 'replication_factor' : 3};
jnosql.cassandra.query.2=CREATE TYPE IF NOT EXISTS library.user
(username text, name text);
jnosql.cassandra.query.3=CREATE TYPE IF NOT EXISTS library.book (id
uuid, title text );
jnosql.cassandra.query.4=CREATE COLUMNFAMILY IF NOT EXISTS
library.rental (id uuid PRIMARY KEY, date text, user user, books
frozen<set<book>>);
```

Compared to key-value, wide-column has more flexibility in the model. But we still have the issue of searching fields that are not an ID; how can we solve this? Let's move on to the following database type to answer this question.

> **Tip**
> Cassandra has a secondary index for allowing querying outside the key. Pay attention because there are several implications for using it.

Document databases

Our third NoSQL type can search for fields aside from the ID; good news! The document NoSQL type has an XML or JSON structure. Searching for the ID is still the more efficient way, but being able to search for information through other fields gives the model more flexibility and makes it easier to explore the information in the database as well.

For this sample, we'll use MongoDB for the implementation. We'll run a single node locally. Please, pay attention when running this in production; but for now, we'll run it from a Docker image:

```
docker run -d --name mongodb-instance -p 27017:27017 mongo
```

As the Maven dependency, we'll add the MongoDB extension:

```
<dependency>
    <groupId>org.eclipse.jnosql.mapping</groupId>
    <artifactId>jnosql-mongodb-extension</artifactId>
    <version>${jnosql.version}</version>
</dependency>
```

In this sample, we'll show the book items inside the store. The model is similar to wide-column in that it is query-driven, but we have more flexibility to search this time. The model follows the DDD principle, with Book as the entity and Author as the value object:

```
@Entity
public class Book {

    @Id
    private String id;

    @Column
    private String title;

    @Column
    private List<String> categories;

    @Column
    private Set<String> languages;

    @Column
    private Author author;

}


  @Entity
public record Author(@Column("nickname") String nickname,
  @Column("name") String name, @Column("profile") String
     profile) {

    public static AuthorBuilder builder() {
        return new AuthorBuilder();
    }
}
```

> **Tip**
>
> If you are using an immutable value object, it is an excellent candidate to use to explore the newest feature from Java: records.

The model is ready to explore; thus, we'll run it on Java SE and explore `DocumentTemplate`, which follows the same principle as the previous database flavors – being a bridge between Java and the database:

```
try (SeContainer container =
  SeContainerInitializer.newInstance().initialize()) {

    Author otavio = Author.builder()
      .nickname("otaviojava").name("Otavio Santana")
        .profile("@otaviojava").build();

    Book cassandra = Book.builder()
            .title("Apache Cassandra Horizontal scalability
              for Java applications")
            .category("database").category("technology")
            .language("Portuguese").language("English")
            .author(otavio).build();

    DocumentTemplate template = container
      .select(DocumentTemplate.class).get();

    template.insert(cassandra);

    System.out.println("The database found: " +
      template.find(Book.class, cassandra.getId()));

    template.delete(Book.class, cassandra.getId());

}
```

The power of documents is similar to relational databases, but we don't have the same powerful transactions as SQL and JOINs. Even with this limitation, we can order elements from any field:

```
try (SeContainer container =
  SeContainerInitializer.newInstance().initialize()) {

    Author neal = Author.builder()
      .nickname("neal").name("Neal Ford")
        .profile("@neal4d").build();
```

```
    Book evolutionary = Book.builder()
            .title("Building Evolutionary Architectures:
              Support Constant Change")
            .category("architecture")
            .category("technology")
            .language("Portuguese").language("English")
            .author(neal).build();
//...
    DocumentTemplate template = container
        .select(DocumentTemplate.class).get();

    template.insert(evolutionary);

    DocumentQuery query = DocumentQuery
        .select().from("Book")
                    .where("author.nickname").eq("neal")
                    .orderBy("title").asc().build();

    System.out.println("The query by API");
    template.select(query).forEach(System.out::println);
}
```

The properties for running the sample will follow the same core idea to take advantage of the twelve-factor app:

```
jnosql.document.database=library
jnosql.mongodb.host=localhost:27017
```

The flexibility the document NoSQL type has in querying is terrific! But what about the relationship between entities? This kind of query is required at some point, so how can we solve it? Let's look at the last NoSQL type and find out.

Graph databases

If you're looking for a relationship, you have come to the right place! Let's talk about graph databases. A graph database is a powerful engine with a graph structure that saves information based on vertices and edges, where an edge is an object to hold the relationship information.

Using an edge, you can define a relationship's direction and properties; it is even more potent than a relational database.

Let's create a simple recommendation engine with a person who can read/write and meet people.

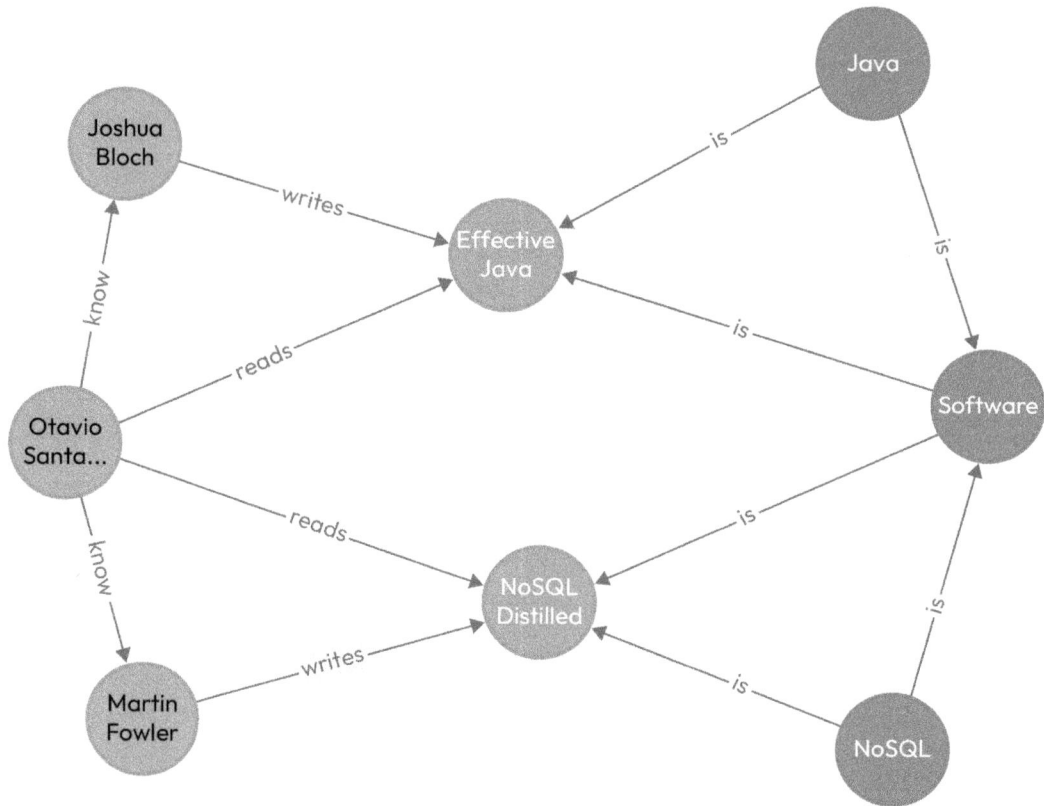

Figure 6.4: The relationships between people and books

The first thing to do is ensure that we have at least a single instance running; remember, this is not the proper way to run in production:

```
docker run --publish=7474:7474 --publish=7687:7687 --env NEO4J_
AUTH=neo4j/admin neo4j
```

We'll have two entities: Book and Person. A person can write N books, read N books, and meet N. A tree hierarchy and a meta-relationship indicate a graph database when we have multiple N-to-N relationships:

```
@Entity
public class Book {

    @Id
    private Long id;
```

```
    @Column
    private String name;

}

@Entity
public class Person {

    @Id
    private Long id;

    @Column
    private String name;

    @Column
    private String profile;
}

@Entity
public class Category {

    @Id
    private Long id;

    @Column
    private String name;

}
```

The graph also has a `GraphTemplate` instance where you can operate with the graph database.

This sample will use a `LibraryGraph` to operate all the operations on this system. Be ready to refactor it as it gets bigger, mainly because it breaks the single responsibility **SOLID** principle.

The main point to remember is the developer's core principle to make the code maintainable and readable; unfortunately, we don't yet have a full set of established best practices for NoSQL as we do with SQL:

```
@ApplicationScoped
class LibraryGraph {

    @Inject
    private GraphTemplate template;
```

```
    public Book save(Book book) {
        Objects.requireNonNull(book, "book is required");
        return template.getTraversalVertex()
          .hasLabel(Book.class)
                .has("name", book.getName())
                .<Book>next()
                .orElseGet(() -> template.insert(book));
    }

    public Category save(Category category) {
        Objects.requireNonNull(category, "category is
          required");
        return template.getTraversalVertex()
          .hasLabel(Category.class)
                .has("name", category.getName())
                .<Category>next()
                .orElseGet(() ->
                    template.insert(category));
    }
//...
    }
```

The last step is to run it. There are tiny differences between the query and operation when inserting entities and relationships. We can implement the following graph using Neo4j.

JNoSQL uses Apache TinkerPop as a communication layer where we can search for queries by using Gremlin. This opens up a world of possibilities:

```
try (SeContainer container =
    SeContainerInitializer.newInstance().initialize()) {

    LibraryGraph graph = container
      .select(LibraryGraph.class).get();

    Category software = graph
      .save(Category.of("Software"));

    Category java = graph.save(Category.of("Java"));

    Person joshua = graph.save(Person.of("Joshua Bloch",
      "@joshbloch"));

    graph.is(java, software);
```

```
graph.write(joshua, effectiveJava);
 List<String> softwareCategories =
   graph.getSubCategories();

List<String> softwareBooks = graph.getSoftwareBooks();

List<String> softwareNoSQLBooks =
  graph.getSoftwareNoSQL();

Set<Category> categories = graph.getCategories(otavio);

Set<String> suggestions = graph.getFollow(otavio);
}
```

The graph database has extensive capabilities to leverage relationships, but it comes at the cost of performance. It is tough to scale the database, and it is slower than a key-value database.

Summary

We've finished our journey through NoSQL types, where we looked at the least flexible to the least scalable types. Paying attention to modeling is crucial because it is different from SQL databases and is a common pitfall for beginners in NoSQL databases.

We introduced you to the JNoSQL Java API standard, which streamlines the integration of Java applications with NoSQL databases. We will discuss Jakarta and the data persistence layer in the chapter on polyglot persistence. In the next chapter, we will cover relational databases using jOOQ.

7

The Missing Guide for jOOQ Adoption

Object-oriented programming (**OOP**) is the most popular approach when discussing enterprise architecture; however, there are more, such as data-driven. In today's data-driven world, jOOQ has emerged as a powerful tool for developers to use to interact with databases, offering a seamless and efficient approach to working with SQL.

Firstly, let's address the fundamental question: what is jOOQ? **jOOQ**, which stands for **Java Object Oriented Querying**, is a lightweight yet robust Java library that empowers developers to write type-safe SQL queries fluently and intuitively. It provides a **domain-specific language** (**DSL**) that encapsulates the complexities of SQL, allowing developers to focus on writing concise and readable code.

Now, you might wonder why jOOQ has gained significant traction among developers. The answer lies in its ability to bridge the gap between the relational world of databases and the object-oriented paradigm of modern application development. jOOQ enables developers to leverage the full power of SQL within their Java code, providing flexibility, performance, and maintainability that is often difficult to achieve with traditional **object-relational mapping** (**ORM**) frameworks.

As we dive deeper into the world of jOOQ, we will explore the concept of data-driven design and its implications. Unlike traditional OOP, which primarily revolves around manipulating objects and their behaviors, data-driven design emphasizes the underlying data structures and their relationships. We will examine how jOOQ embraces this approach, empowering developers to efficiently handle complex database interactions while maintaining the benefits of strong typing and compile-time safety.

In this chapter, we will explore the jOOQ framework and how to use it in an enterprise architecture with both Jakarta EE and MicroProfile:

- Data-driven and object-oriented programming in Java
- What is jOOQ?
- Using jOOQ with Jakarta/MicroProfile

So, let's embark on this journey to discover the power of jOOQ and understand how it revolutionizes how we interact with databases, bridging the gap between the world of SQL and OOP.

Technical requirements

The following are required for this chapter:

- Java 17

- Git

- Maven

- Any preferred IDE

- The code for this chapter can be found at: `https://github.com/PacktPublishing/Persistence-Best-Practices-for-Java-Applications/tree/main/chapter-07`

Data-driven and object-oriented programming in Java

In Java, **data-driven** programming refers to an approach where the underlying data and its structure primarily drive the design and functionality of a program. It focuses on manipulating and processing data in a way that allows for flexibility, extensibility, and easy modification without heavily relying on the behavior of objects.

In contrast, OOP is a programming paradigm that revolves around objects, which are instances of classes. OOP emphasizes encapsulating data and related behavior within objects, promoting concepts such as inheritance, polymorphism, and abstraction. It focuses on modeling real-world entities as objects and defining their behaviors through methods and relationships.

The critical difference between data-driven programming and OOP lies in their approach to program design. In OOP, the emphasis is on modeling entities and their behavior, organizing code around objects and their interactions. This approach works well when the behavior of objects is complex or when there is a need to represent the real-world entities in the system.

On the other hand, data-driven programming prioritizes manipulating and processing data structures. It is beneficial when dealing with large amounts of data, such as databases or data-centric applications. Data-driven programming allows for efficient querying, filtering, and transformation of data, often leveraging declarative approaches such as SQL or other query languages.

In some situations, a data-driven approach may be more suitable than an object-oriented one. Here are a few examples:

- **Data processing and analysis**: A data-driven approach with specialized libraries or frameworks can offer better performance and flexibility when dealing with extensive datasets or performing complex analytical tasks

- **Database-driven applications**: When developing applications that interact heavily with databases or rely on data from external sources, a data-driven approach such as jOOQ can simplify database interactions and optimize query execution

- **Configuration-driven systems**: In systems where the behavior is primarily determined by configuration files or external data, a data-driven approach allows easy modifications and customization without requiring code changes

- **Rule-based systems**: In applications that involve complex rule evaluation or decision-making based on data, a data-driven approach can provide a transparent and manageable way to express and process rules

It's important to note that OOP and data-driven programming are not mutually exclusive, and they can often be combined to achieve the desired functionality and maintainability in a Java application. The choice between the two approaches depends on the specific requirements of the system and the nature of the problem being solved.

While data-driven programming offers several advantages, it also comes with inevitable trade-offs. Here are some of the trade-offs associated with data-driven programming:

- **Increased complexity**: Data-driven programming can introduce additional complexity, especially when dealing with large and complex data structures. Managing and manipulating data at a granular level may require intricate code and logic, making the system harder to understand and maintain.

- **Reduced encapsulation**: In data-driven programming, the focus is primarily on the data and its manipulation rather than encapsulating behavior within objects. This can lead to reduced encapsulation and increased data exposure, potentially compromising the security and integrity of the system.

- **Limited expressiveness**: While data-driven programming provides powerful data manipulation and querying mechanisms, it may have limitations when expressing complex business logic or relationships between data. OOP, emphasizing behavior and encapsulation, can often provide more expressive and intuitive solutions for such scenarios.

Despite these trade-offs, data-driven programming can be highly beneficial when efficient data manipulation, querying, and flexibility are crucial. By understanding these trade-offs, developers can make informed decisions when choosing between object-oriented and data-driven approaches, considering their applications' specific requirements and constraints.

Object-oriented is the most popular paradigm when discussing enterprise applications; however, we can explore more paradigms, such as a data-driven design.

> **Note**
>
> This chapter gives a brief overview of this topic, but if you want to go deep, there are two recommended materials.
>
> The first one is the book *Data-Oriented Programming* by Yehonathan Sharvit, which talks about this pattern, for which we can summarize three principles:
>
> - The code is data-separated
> - Data is immutable
> - Data has flexible access
>
> The second one is an article called *Data-Oriented Programming* by Brian Goetz, where Brian explains more about new features of Java, mainly records, and how to take advantage of Java.
>
> Given this overview of data-oriented programming, let's go deep with one of the most popular frameworks that can help you to design and create data-oriented applications: jOOQ.

What is jOOQ?

jOOQ is a powerful Java library that bridges the gap between OOP and data-oriented programming in the context of enterprise applications. While OOP has long been the dominant paradigm in developing enterprise applications, there are cases where a data-oriented approach can offer unique advantages. jOOQ provides an elegant solution for developers to use to harness the power of SQL and leverage data-driven design principles within their Java code.

OOP has been widely adopted for its ability to model complex systems by encapsulating data and behavior within objects. It emphasizes code organization, reusability, and modularity. However, as enterprise applications deal with vast amounts of data and complex database interactions, a purely object-oriented approach can sometimes be limiting.

This is where jOOQ comes into play. jOOQ enables developers to seamlessly integrate SQL and relational database operations into their Java code. It provides a fluent, type-safe, and intuitive DSL for constructing SQL queries and interacting with databases. By embracing a data-oriented approach, jOOQ empowers developers to work directly with data structures and leverage the full power of SQL for querying, aggregating, and transforming data.

With jOOQ, developers can break free from the constraints of traditional ORM frameworks and gain fine-grained control over their database interactions. By embracing a data-oriented mindset, they can optimize performance, handle complex data manipulations, and take advantage of the features and optimizations offered by the underlying database system.

By using jOOQ, developers can tap into the benefits of OOP and data-oriented programming paradigms. They can continue to utilize the proven principles of object-oriented design for encapsulating behavior within objects while also benefiting from the efficiency and flexibility of data-oriented programming for handling large datasets and complex database operations.

In the following sections, we will explore the features and capabilities of jOOQ in greater detail. We will delve into the DSL provided by jOOQ for constructing SQL queries, discuss its integration with Java code, and showcase its benefits for data-driven design. Together, we will discover how jOOQ can revolutionize how we interact with databases and enable a seamless fusion of OOP and data-oriented programming in enterprise applications.

While jOOQ offers many benefits and advantages, it also has inevitable trade-offs. Here are some of the trade-offs associated with using jOOQ:

- **Learning curve**: jOOQ introduces a new DSL for constructing SQL queries, which requires developers to familiarize themselves with its syntax and concepts. There is a learning curve involved in understanding the intricacies of jOOQ and utilizing it effectively.

- **Increased code complexity**: Using jOOQ can introduce additional code complexity compared to traditional ORM frameworks or direct SQL queries. The DSL syntax and the need to map between Java objects and database records may result in more code and potential complexity, especially for complex database interactions.

- **Limited database portability**: jOOQ generates SQL queries based on the underlying database dialect and its specific features. While jOOQ aims to provide a unified API across different databases, some differences in supported features and behavior may still exist. It can limit the portability of code between other database systems.

- **Performance considerations**: While jOOQ offers efficient query construction and execution, the performance may still be influenced by factors such as database schema design, indexing, and query optimization. It is crucial to consider the performance implications of jOOQ-generated queries and optimize the database schema accordingly.

- **Maintenance and upgrades**: As with any third-party library, using jOOQ introduces a dependency that needs to be managed and maintained. Keeping up with new releases, compatibility with different Java versions, and resolving potential issues or bugs may require additional effort during maintenance and upgrades.

- **Limited abstraction of an underlying database**: Unlike ORM frameworks that provide a higher level of abstraction, jOOQ requires developers to understand SQL and the underlying database schema well. It may be a disadvantage if you prefer a more abstract approach with hidden database-specific details.

- **Potential impedance mismatch**: There may be cases where the object-oriented nature of the application clashes with the data-oriented approach of jOOQ. Balancing the two paradigms and maintaining consistency between the object model and the database schema can be challenging and may require careful design considerations.

While jOOQ provides powerful capabilities for data-driven programming in Java, there may be better choices in some situations. It's essential to weigh these trade-offs against your project's specific requirements and constraints. Consider project complexity, team experience, performance needs, and database requirements when deciding whether jOOQ is the right tool for your application.

When we talk about a new tool, we compare it with the one we know; thus, let's discuss more the difference between jOOQ and the **Java Persistence API (JPA)** and when we should choose one over the other.

JPA versus jOOQ

Both jOOQ and JPA are popular choices for database access in Java applications, but they have different approaches and use cases. Here is a comparison between the two and when you might choose one over the other:

jOOQ

- **SQL-centric approach**: jOOQ provides a fluent DSL that allows developers to construct SQL queries in a type-safe and intuitive manner. It gives fine-grained control over the SQL statements and allows leveraging the full power of SQL. jOOQ is well suited to scenarios where complex querying, database-specific features, and performance optimizations are essential.

- **Data-driven design**: jOOQ embraces a data-oriented programming paradigm, making it suitable for working with large datasets and intricate database operations. It provides efficient data manipulation capabilities and allows developers to work closely with the underlying data structures. jOOQ is a good fit for applications with central data processing and analysis.

- **Database-specific features**: jOOQ supports various database-specific features and functions, allowing developers to take advantage of the specific capabilities offered by different database systems. It makes it a suitable choice when working closely with a particular database and using its unique features.

JPA

- **ORM**: JPA focuses on mapping Java objects to relational database tables, providing a higher level of abstraction. It allows developers to work with persistent entities and automatically maps objects to database records. JPA is a good fit for applications that heavily rely on object-oriented design and require a seamless integration between objects and the database.

- **Cross-database portability**: JPA aims to provide a portable API that can work with different databases. It abstracts away database-specific details, allowing applications to switch between database systems with minimal code changes. JPA is a suitable choice when you need flexibility regarding the database backend and want to avoid vendor lock-in.

- **Rapid application development**: JPA offers features such as automatic CRUD operations, caching, and transaction management, simplifying and accelerating application development. It provides a higher level of abstraction, reducing the need for writing low-level SQL queries. JPA is beneficial when you prioritize rapid prototyping, productivity, and a focus on business logic over database-specific optimizations.

Choosing between jOOQ and JPA depends on your specific project requirements. If your application is data-intensive, requires complex querying, and needs fine-grained control over SQL, jOOQ might be a better choice. On the other hand, JPA may be the more suitable option if you prioritize object-oriented design, portability across different databases, and rapid application development. It's also worth considering hybrid approaches where you can use both jOOQ and JPA together in different parts of your application, leveraging the strengths of each library as needed.

Given an introduction about jOOQ, let's put this into practice, this time combined with Jakarta EE. This book shows Jakarta EE in several persistence frameworks; in this chapter, we'll show you Jakarta EE with jOOQ.

Using jOOQ with Jakarta/MicroProfile

In this section, we will explore the integration of jOOQ with Jakarta EE and MicroProfile, two powerful frameworks in the Java ecosystem. jOOQ, with its data-driven approach and SQL-centric capabilities, can seamlessly complement the enterprise-grade features provided by Jakarta EE and the microservices-oriented practice of MicroProfile. By combining these technologies, developers can unlock a powerful toolkit for building robust, scalable, and data-driven Java applications.

Jakarta EE, formerly Java EE, is a set of specifications and APIs that provides a standardized platform for building enterprise applications in Java. It offers a wide range of features, including servlets, **JavaServer Faces (JSF)**, **Enterprise JavaBeans (EJB)**, and JPA. Developers can leverage a mature ecosystem and industry standards with Jakarta EE to create scalable and maintainable applications.

On the other hand, MicroProfile is a community-driven initiative that focuses on building microservices-based applications in Java. It provides a lightweight and modular set of specifications and APIs tailored for microservice architectures. MicroProfile enables developers to leverage technologies such as JAX-RS, JSON-P, and CDI in microservices, allowing for greater flexibility and agility.

Combining jOOQ with Jakarta EE and MicroProfile can bring the best of both worlds to your Java applications. Here are some benefits and use cases of this combination:

- **Enhanced database interactions**: jOOQ's SQL-centric approach allows you to write complex and optimized SQL queries directly in your Java code. It enables efficient and fine-grained control over database interactions, allowing for optimized data retrieval, updates, and analysis. Integrating jOOQ with Jakarta EE and MicroProfile will enable you to seamlessly leverage jOOQ's powerful query-building capabilities within your enterprise or microservices applications.

- **Data-driven microservices**: Architectures often require efficient data access and manipulation across multiple services. Combining jOOQ with MicroProfile allows you to design microservices that leverage jOOQ's data-driven approach for seamless database integration. It enables each microservice to independently handle its data operations, benefiting from the performance and flexibility offered by jOOQ's DSL.

- **Integration with JPA and ORM**: Jakarta EE applications often utilize JPA and ORM frameworks for database interactions. By integrating jOOQ with Jakarta EE and its persistence capabilities, you can leverage the benefits of both jOOQ's SQL-centric approach and JPA's object-oriented design. It allows you to efficiently handle complex queries and leverage JPA's entity management, transactions, and caching features, resulting in a powerful and flexible data access layer.

- **Cross-cutting concerns and scalability**: Jakarta EE and MicroProfile provide a wealth of features for cross-cutting concerns such as security, logging, and monitoring. By integrating jOOQ with these frameworks, you can leverage their capabilities to ensure consistent security policies, efficient logging, and monitoring of database interactions across your application or microservices architecture.

Throughout this section, we will explore practical examples and demonstrate how to combine jOOQ with Jakarta EE and MicroProfile effectively. We will showcase the integration of jOOQ with Jakarta EE's Persistence API, illustrate the use of jOOQ in microservices architectures with MicroProfile, and discuss best practices for leveraging the combined power of these technologies.

By the end of this section, you will have a solid understanding of how to work with jOOQ, Jakarta EE, and MicroProfile together, enabling you to build robust and data-driven Java applications in enterprise and microservices contexts. Let's dive in and explore the possibilities of this powerful combination.

To demonstrate the combination potential, we'll create a simple project using Java SE with Maven, but as a highlight, we can convert this code smoothly into microservices. This project is a CRUD with a single table, `Book`, where we'll execute operations within, as in an executable class.

We'll still use a simple database project, the H2, to reduce our project's requirements. But you can replace it on production with PostgreSQL, MariaDB, and so on. Indeed, that is the beauty of relational databases; we can change easier between databases without much impact if we compare them with NoSQL databases:

1. Let's start with the configurations on the Maven project, where we'll include the dependencies:

```
<dependency>
    <groupId>org.jboss.weld.se</groupId>
    <artifactId>weld-se-shaded</artifactId>
    <version>${weld.se.core.version}</version>
</dependency>
<dependency>
    <groupId>io.smallrye.config</groupId>
    <artifactId>smallrye-config-core</artifactId>
    <version>2.13.0</version>
</dependency>
<dependency>
    <groupId>org.jooq</groupId>
    <artifactId>jooq</artifactId>
    <version>3.18.4</version>
</dependency>
```

```
    </dependency>
    <dependency>
        <groupId>com.h2database</groupId>
        <artifactId>h2</artifactId>
        <version>2.1.214</version>
    </dependency>
    <dependency>
        <groupId>org.apache.commons</groupId>
        <artifactId>commons-dbcp2</artifactId>
        <version>2.9.0</version>
    </dependency>
```

2. After the Maven dependencies, the next step is to include the plugins to generate the database structure and then create the jOOQ based on this table. We'll start the data structure and, using the plugin, we'll execute the following query; as you'll see, we'll make the schema and include some books in it. We'll not show the plugin source code; see the repository source for more details:

```
DROP TABLE IF EXISTS book
;
CREATE TABLE book (
                    id INT NOT NULL,
                    title VARCHAR(400) NOT NULL,
                    author VARCHAR(400) NOT NULL,
                    release INT,

                    CONSTRAINT pk_t_book PRIMARY KEY (id)
)
;

INSERT INTO book VALUES (1, 'Fundamentals of Software
  Architecture', 'Neal Ford' , 2020)
;

INSERT INTO book VALUES (2, 'Staff Engineer:
  Leadership beyond the management track', 'Will
    Larson' , 2021)
;

INSERT INTO book VALUES (3, 'Building Evolutionary
  Architectures', 'Neal Ford' , 2017)
;

INSERT INTO book VALUES (4, 'Clean Code', 'Robert
  Cecil Martin' , 2008)
```

```
;

INSERT INTO book VALUES (5, 'Patterns of Enterprise
  Application Architecture', 'Martin Fowler' , 2002)
;
```

3. The Maven infrastructure is ready, and the next step is to define the configuration to get the connection to the database and make it available to the CDI context. We'll combine Jakarta CDI with Eclipse MicroProfile Config and extract the properties such as the JDBC URL and credentials.

4. We'll put this credentials information, such as the username and password, in `microprofile-config.properties`; however, remember that you should not do so with production credentials. One thing I do is overwrite those configurations by the environment. Thus, the developer will understand this at production without knowing about it; a developer knows about those properties without comprehending the production properties. This is one of the advantages of taking the implementation to the edge of the Twelve-Factor App (`https://12factor.net`):

```
@ApplicationScoped
class ConnectionSupplier {

    private static final Logger LOGGER = Logger
      .getLogger(ConnectionSupplier.class.getName());
    private static final String URL= "db.url";

    private static final String USER = "db.username";

    private static final String PASSWORD =
      "db.password";

    private static final Config CONFIG =
      ConfigProvider.getConfig();


    @ApplicationScoped
    @Produces
    public Connection get() throws SQLException {
        LOGGER.fine("Starting the database
          connection");
        var url = CONFIG.getValue(URL, String.class);
        var password =
          CONFIG.getOptionalValue(PASSWORD,
            String.class).orElse("");
        var user = CONFIG.getValue(USER,
          String.class);
```

```
          return DriverManager.getConnection(
            url, user, password);
      }

      public void close(@Disposes Connection connection)
        throws SQLException {
          connection.close();
          LOGGER.fine("closing the database
            connection");
      }

  }
```

5. CDI can create and destroy bean instances in your container context. We'll use this to develop and close connections, avoiding any connection leaks in our application. Once we have the connection, let's create the DSLContext instance – this is the bridge between our data and Java, providing an easy and safe way through fluent-API:

```
@ApplicationScoped
class ContextSupplier implements Supplier<DSLContext> {

    private final Connection connection;

    @Inject
    ContextSupplier(Connection connection) {
        this.connection = connection;
    }

    @Override
    @Produces
    public DSLContext get() {
        return using(connection, SQLDialect.H2);
    }
}
```

6. We could make both Connection and DSLContext available and handled by CDI; the next step is using both to work with the relational database. You could inject DSLContext as a field, but since we have created it using Java SE, we'll create a SeContainer and select it, as in the following code:

```
try (SeContainer container =
  SeContainerInitializer.newInstance().initialize()) {
    DSLContext context =
      container.select(DSLContext.class).get();
//...
}
```

7. Are you ready for action? Let's do a CRUD operation without creating an entity thanks to jOOQ, which, based on the database schema, will generate the data structure we can work with. The first step in the operation is the insertion. The code shows the record creation where we can set attributes and store them based on the setter methods:

```
BookRecord record = context.newRecord(BOOK);
record.setId(random.nextInt(0, 100));
record.setRelease(2022);
record.setAuthor("Otavio Santana");
record.setTitle("Apache Cassandra Horizontal
  scalability for Java applications");
record.store();
```

8. With the data, we can read that information from the database; using fluent-API and the `select` method with the `DSLContext` class, we can do several select query operations. The query will select the books ordered by title. The advantage of this approach is that we'll see whether the query is compatible at the application level most of the time because it won't compile if you do any irregular operation:

```
Result<Record> books = context.select()
        .from(BOOK)
        .orderBy(BOOK.TITLE)
        .fetch();

books.forEach(book -> {
    var id = book.getValue(BOOK.ID);
    var author = book.getValue(BOOK.AUTHOR);
    var title = book.getValue(BOOK.TITLE);
    var release = book.getValue(BOOK.RELEASE);

    System.out.printf("Book %s by %s has id: %d and
      release: %d%n",
            title, author, id, release);
});
```

9. The last two steps are `update` and `delete`; you can execute the other operations, exploring the fluent-API capability. We can define as many parameters and conditions as we wish. The sample we're using will set the `where` condition at the `ID` value:

```
context.update(BOOK)
        .set(BOOK.TITLE, "Cassandra Horizontal
          scalability for Java applications")
        .where(BOOK.ID.eq(randomId))
```

```
            .execute();

context.delete(BOOK)
        .where(BOOK.ID.eq(randomId))
        .execute();
```

We could explore the whole CRUD operation based on the data without creating entities thanks to the jOOQ API. The data approach allows for generating the structure from the schema. We can guarantee that my application will work with the last entity without needing any work. That ends our jOOQ journey for today.

Summary

This chapter delved into data-driven programming and its trade-offs compared to the object-oriented approach. We explored the benefits and challenges of embracing a data-driven mindset, understanding that there are scenarios where a data-oriented approach can provide unique advantages over the traditional object-oriented paradigm. We then witnessed how jOOQ, a powerful Java library, bridges the gap between OOP and data-driven programming, allowing developers to leverage the full power of SQL and data manipulation within their Java code.

We also examined the integration of jOOQ with Jakarta EE and MicroProfile, two frameworks widely used in developing enterprise and microservices applications. By combining these technologies, developers can take advantage of both the data-driven capabilities of jOOQ and the enterprise-grade features provided by Jakarta EE and the microservices-oriented approach of MicroProfile. This integration enables efficient database interactions, fine-grained control over SQL queries, and the ability to leverage object-oriented and data-oriented design principles in a unified architecture.

By combining the data-driven approach enabled by jOOQ with the enterprise-grade features of Jakarta EE and MicroProfile, and exploring the groundbreaking capabilities of MicroStream, we can take our applications to new heights of performance, scalability, and efficiency. We are on the brink of a new era in database-driven application development, where the power of data meets the speed of execution.

So, let's embark on the next chapter of our journey, where we dive into the world of MicroStream and unleash the true potential of our persistence layer, Jakarta EE, and MicroProfile-powered applications. Exciting times lie ahead as we embrace this cutting-edge technology and witness the transformation it brings to our development process and the performance of our applications.

8

Ultra-Fast In-Memory
Persistence with Eclipse Store

NoSQL and SQL databases can be impressive and powerful when handling their target use cases. However, users seeking optimal performance need to be aware of other aspects that can influence the application in terms of processing efficiency, speed, and even code design. In this regard, one example can be mentioned upfront: most of these database solutions will require some sort of mapping between the database schema and the application data models. As you can imagine, the mapping needs to happen every single time data flows back and forth between the application and the database. This characteristic, known as **object-relational impedance mismatch**, has a high potential to impact most of the database types we've mentioned so far – SQL and NoSQL.

In this chapter, we will discuss another database paradigm, in-memory databases. Adding to the significant performance boost, this is definitely the type of database to be leveraged when working on use cases such as data processing, web and mobile apps, and caching and real-time analytics. For such scenarios, a highly performant data storage solution, low-latency data access, and real-time data processing appear to be promising alternatives since they allow for the delivery of super-fast persistence solutions.

We'll explore the aforementioned concepts with **Eclipse Store**, a high-performance, lightweight solution for in-memory persistence. One of the points of this database is to be faster and eliminate extra processing, and reduce code size and complexity, especially when compared with the integration of, for example, SQL databases and Hibernate/JPA.

In this chapter, we will cover the following main topics:

- Why is latency secretly added to every database operation? We will understand what object-relational impedance mismatch is and how it can affect persistence performance.

- What is an in-memory persistence storage and how does it differ from other database types?

- Exploring Eclipse Store.

- Eclipse Store with Jakarta/MicroProfile.

Technical requirements

The following are the technical requirements for this chapter:

- Java 17

- Git

- Maven

- Any preferred IDE

The source code for this chapter is available at `https://github.com/PacktPublishing/Persistence-Best-Practices-for-Java-Applications/tree/main/chapter-08`.

Object-relational impedance mismatch explained

As Java developers, we know the power of the **object-oriented programming (OOP)** paradigm – it allows us to explore several patterns based on polymorphism, encapsulation, heritage, interface, creating custom types, and so on. We love it! Mainly because we can combine these approaches with design patterns to create clean and readable code.

Unfortunately, many of these OOP concepts and behaviors are not available on the database side, a characteristic named **impedance mismatch**.

Object-Relational Mapping (ORM) impedance mismatch is a specific type of impedance mismatch that occurs when mapping data between an oop language and a **relational database management system (RDBMS)**.

OOP languages such as Java, Python, and C# use objects to represent and manipulate data, whereas relational databases use tables to store and manage data. ORM is a technique used to bridge the gap between these two different paradigms by mapping objects to database tables and vice versa.

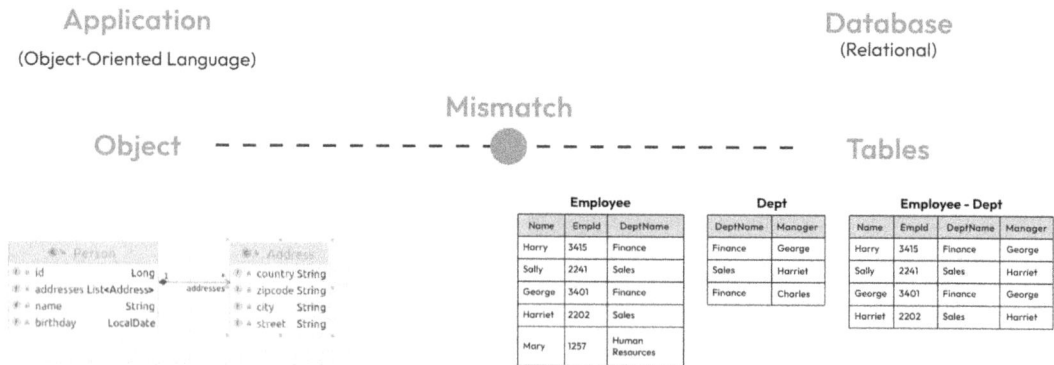

Figure 8.1 – Example of Java object model equivalent mapping on the database schema

The ORM impedance mismatch occurs because objects and tables have different properties and structures. For example, objects can have complex data types, inheritance, and polymorphism, while tables consist of simple rows and columns. In addition, objects can have relationships with other entities, whereas tables have relationships between rows.

To mitigate this impedance mismatch and make the developer more efficient, ORM tools provide mapping strategies that allow developers to map objects to tables and vice versa. These strategies can include ORM patterns such as table inheritance, association mapping, and lazy loading.

Despite these strategies, ORM impedance mismatch can still occur due to differences in the query language, performance issues, and scalability problems. As a result, developers need to be aware of the limitations and trade-offs involved in using ORM tools and consider alternative solutions where necessary.

Another item to highlight in regard to the mapping processing is that it uses a mapper. The mapper, used on every app-database interaction, is responsible for converting to/from entities and requires a lot of CPU power, which may end up being heavier than the executed query itself.

This mapper has a bright mechanism for communicating between paradigms. Even with a cache and the most advanced techniques to improve performance, this process might be a nightmare in several applications.

A technology we can adopt to beat this challenge and avoid doing extra Java processing on every database operation is Eclipse Store. Let's get into what this in-memory database is, how it works, and how you can get started with it.

Eclipse Store is a Java-based, open source, in-memory data storage technology that offers a new approach to object persistence.

Unlike traditional databases that rely on ORM to map objects to relational tables, Eclipse Store's internal mechanisms locate and use Java objects available on the heap. It can get the information *directly* from memory, eliminating the need for mapping or serialization. This approach results in faster application performance since it avoids the ORM impedance mismatch and reduces the need for costly database access.

Eclipse Store began as MicroStream 10 years ago as a closed source project. Recently, MicroStream went open source and became two Eclipse projects, one being Eclipse Store.

Eclipse Store provides a Java API that allows developers to store, load, and manipulate Java objects directly in memory without the need to access a separate database. The data can optionally be persisted externally, and in such cases, it is stored in a compressed binary format, allowing for efficient memory resource use. This approach eliminates the need for ORM, which can be time-consuming and resource-intensive, especially for complex object hierarchies.

Eclipse Store operates mostly in memory; therefore, it can provide ultra-fast read and write access to data, making it ideal for high-performance data-processing applications, such as real-time analytics, financial trading, and gaming.

In addition to its speed and performance benefits, Eclipse Store offers a high degree of flexibility and scalability. It supports distributed data structures, allowing data to be distributed across multiple nodes and integrated with other databases or data sources.

Overall, Eclipse Store provides a compelling alternative to traditional ORM-based databases, offering faster performance and reduced complexity for applications that require ultra-fast data processing.

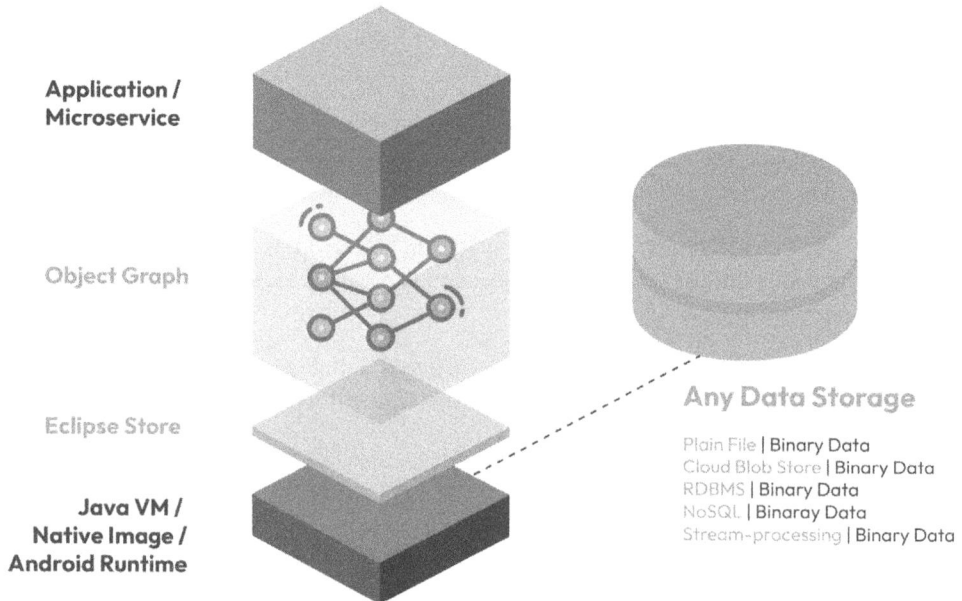

Figure 8.2 – Architecture overview of Eclipse Store

Applications using Eclipse Store as the in-memory data storage solution can rely on the following:

- **Fast performance**: Integrate fast and efficiently, relying on quick read and write operations without the extra overhead of an ORM tool.

- **In-memory storage**: Fast access to data, as it is obtained directly from the memory heap.

- **Easy to use**: Developers can quickly get up to speed as the technology is designed to be simple and easy to use, with a familiar Java syntax and optional annotations that make it easy to define and persist data.

- **No external dependencies**: Using it is pretty simple as the only dependency you'll need is Eclipse Store (which basically depends on a logging library). You should have no concerns regarding library conflicts or compatibility issues.

- **Lightweight**: A data storage solution that doesn't require a lot of resources or configuration, and is easy to set up and deploy.

- **Flexibility**: Choose from all of the data types (with very few exceptions), and use it in various application sizes – from small-scale projects to enterprise-level systems.

- **Open source**: Eclipse Store is offered in multiple types, one of them being a free open source project, meaning unlimited usage and customization that can meet your specific needs.

- **High availability**: When used, it provides built-in high availability and redundancy features, ensuring your data is always available and protected.

- **Scalability**: Easily add more nodes or resources to handle increasing data volumes, as the database is designed from scratch to meet such goals.

In the following sections, we'll drill down into this powerful and flexible solution for in-memory data management and persistence that can help developers build fast and efficient applications. Let's learn about the basics of Eclipse Store, go through code examples, and understand how to create an ultra-fast application with a modern, cloud-native, in-memory, open source solution.

In-memory persistence storage – Eclipse Store

Eclipse Store is a data storage solution that is fast due to the removal of the mapping process, the parse operation on queries, avoiding drawbacks of traditional query execution, and using a unique and advanced serialization process. Eclipse Store estimates that 90% of the query time is based on these operations.

The benchmarks (https://eclipsestore.io/) show results that can be up to **1,000 times faster** than a SQL database with JPA. Positive aspects from a developer perspective are the short learning curve and the simplicity of installation and use.

To get started, the first step is to install Eclipse Store, which is as simple as adding a dependency to your application's Maven configuration.

Some key points of this solution include achieving lightning-fast in-memory data processing using pure Java, with the capability for microsecond query times, low-latency data access, and handling massive data workloads. This approach enables significant savings in CPU power, reduces CO_2 emissions, and lowers costs within data centers.

Memory is volatile; therefore, in order to behave as a persistent storage, data must be stored somewhere else. Eclipse Store's default storage target is the filesystem, in a local folder. That's a good option to start with, but thinking of production needs, you'll probably want to save your data in different locations.

The good news is you can choose from over 15 different options: the storage targets (`https://docs.microstream.one/manual/storage/storage-targets/index.html`) range from relational databases to NoSQL databases, as well as blob services. Examples would be MariaDB, PostgreSQL, Redis, and Amazon S3.

Another possibility unlocked by using this technology that you may enjoy as well is that you can now create a custom graph structure as per your business needs and query with pure Java (no need to use SQL and similar!), decreasing the cognitive load for developers.

You can use Eclipse Store with several runtime technologies, such as Helidon, Spring, and Quarkus. In this book, we explain how to use it relying only on CDI; in other words, you'll learn how to use the technology independent of the vendor or platform it is going to be integrated with. Once we get up to speed on the basics using only the Java standard APIs, we should be able to start trying out different Jakarta EE and MicroProfile vendors, such as Helidon, Wildfly, and Payara.

In our context, CDI acts as the glue between our enterprise's architectural components. Thus, it is the mechanism that enables you to inject Eclipse Store as a library, a component, a module, and so on. Let's get started now with seeing how to persist and manage data using in-memory database storage and CDI.

The basics of how to store and manage data in memory

To explain Eclipse Store further, let's see it in action: we'll create our first example with Java SE and CDI. The goal of this example is to demonstrate how to create a smooth CRUD process for a car, where each car should hold its model, make, and year as attributes.

First things first – create a simple Maven project using `maven-archetype-quickstart`. Installing Eclipse Store is simple; all you need is to add its dependencies to the Maven project. See an example of `pom.xml` as follows:

```xml
<dependency>
    <groupId>one.microstream</groupId>
    <artifactId>eclipse-store-integrations-cdi</artifactId>
    <version>07.00.00-MS-GA</version>
</dependency>
<dependency>
    <groupId>org.jboss.weld.se</groupId>
    <artifactId>weld-se-shaded</artifactId>
    <version>3.1.9.Final</version>
</dependency>
<dependency>
    <groupId>io.smallrye.config</groupId>
    <artifactId>smallrye-config</artifactId>
    <version>2.7.0</version>
</dependency>
```

Once the dependency is set, we can start coding. The following Java class, the Car entity, is our data model. As per Eclipse Store's recommendation, the attributes should be defined as final, resulting in an immutable class:

```
public class Car {

    private final String plate;
    private final Year year;
    private final String make;
    private final String model;
    // add getters and setters
    // they are removed here for brevity
}
```

The next step is to create the graph or structure to hold the data and provide it to us. To represent the collection of cars, we'll create a Garage repository where all data manipulation should happen.

You're free to manipulate a car's data or to create any other new data structure; you code it using pure Java and leave it to Eclipse Store to handle the rest. The only required component we must use is the identification of this Garage as a structure. To do so, annotate it with the @Storage annotation.

The @Storage annotation indicates the root object of the graph that will be handled by Eclipse Store. In this case, Garage is our root object:

```
@Storage
public class Garage {

    private List<Car> cars;

    public Garage() {
        this.cars = new ArrayList<>();
    }

    public void add(Car car) {
        this.cars.add(car);
    }

    public List<Car> getCars() {
        return this.cars.stream()
          .collect(Collectors.toUnmodifiableList());
    }

    public Optional<Car> findByModel(String model) {
        return this.cars.stream().filter(c ->
```

```
        c.getModel().equals(model))
            .findFirst();
    }
}
```

This example covers all the required code and dependencies for us to be able to use `Garage` to add and find cars by model. And it only uses Java SE, no specific runtime!

Moving forward, we'll cover the second sample focusing on the service layer, where we'll implement the validation of the entity's data before it is moved to storage. This validation is pretty straightforward; we'll check whether `car` is `null`.

In order to manipulate the `cars` data, we'll need an instance of `Garage` in our `CarService`. To use CDI to provide us with an instance of this class, we can use the `@Inject` annotation from CDI.

When executing a database operation, we would probably want it to happen in a transaction, right? Yes, in the relational database maybe. Here, we rely on the `@Store` annotation to configure which methods should be allowed to change the data structure. Observe the `public void add (Car car)` method as follows and its annotation:

```
@ApplicationScoped
public class CarService {

    @Inject
    private Garage garage;

    @Store
    public void add(Car car) {
        Objects.requireNonNull(car, "car is required");
        this.garage.add(car);
    }

    public List<Car> getCars() {
        return this.garage.getCars();
    }

    public Optional<Car> findByModel(String model) {
        Objects.requireNonNull(model, "model is required");
        return this.garage.findByModel(model);
    }
}
```

Great, we have enough code at this point in order to test it out and have some fun, so let's execute it! To consume our `CarService` APIs, we'll need a new class, which we can call App, and a `public` `static void main(final String[] args)` method. In the first couple of lines of the code demonstrated next, notice the following:

- The service API that retrieves the list of all the cars, `service.getCars()`

- The search operation invoked by the service API, `service.findByModel("Corolla")`

When running the code for the first time, you'll observe in the output logs that the retrieved cars list will be empty; however, when you run it twice, you can see the data:

```java
public static void main(final String[] args) {
    try (SeContainer container =
      SeContainerInitializer.newInstance().initialize()) {
        final CarService service =
          container.select(CarService.class).get();

        System.out.println("The current car list: " +
          service.getCars());

        Optional<Car> model =
          service.findByModel("Corolla");

        System.out.println("Entity found: " + model);

        Car dodge = Car.builder()
                .make("Dodge")
                .model("Wagon")
                .year(Year.of(1993))
                .plate("JN8AE2KP7D9956349").build();

        Car ford = Car.builder()
                .make("Ford")
                .model("F250")
                .year(Year.of(2005))
                .plate("WBANE73577B200053").build();

        Car honda = Car.builder()
                .make("Honda")
                .model("S2000")
                .year(Year.of(2005))
                .plate("WBANE73577B200053").build();

        Car toyota = Car.builder()
                .make("Toyota")
                .model("Corolla")
```

```
                    .year(Year.of(2005))
                    .plate("WBANE73577B200053").build();

        service.add(ford);
        service.add(honda);
        service.add(toyota);
        service.add(dodge);


    }
    System.exit(0);
}
```

If you try running this code a couple of times, you may notice that around the third try, it looks like the items are getting duplicated! This is a behavior of our list object, which can be easily adjusted to solve this behavior. Update the structure to a Set instead of List and ensure that the Car entity has the equals and hashcode implemented adequately.

The application's properties file holds the settings configuration for the *directory* and the *number of threads* used in the engine. The possibility to externalize this configuration is facilitated by to the integration with *Eclipse MicroProfile Configuration* (https://download.eclipse. org/microprofile/microprofile-config-3.0/microprofile-config-spec-3.0.html). We saw a similar configuration approach in the previous chapter about JNoSQL, as it relies on the same underlying configuration mechanism:

```
one.Eclipse Store.storage.directory=target/data
one.Eclipse Store.channel.count=4
```

Pretty simple, right? Before we move forward, let's understand the importance of the second setting listed previously, one.Eclipse Store.channel.count. This in-memory solution can be fine-tuned in multiple ways, one of them being adjusting the number of channels (threads) that the engine can use to execute I/O operations. This configuration should always be configured with a value equal to 2^n.

Externalizing the configuration with specification-based approaches facilitates service maintenance. It should require very little effort when changing your application implementation, as you'll notice in the upcoming section when we create a microservice based on this sample code. The reason for the simplified maintenance is that the chosen in-memory database storage, Eclipse Store, uses CDI, which happens to also be the core engine for both MicroProfile and Jakarta EE.

After exploring how to configure and implement a service that relies on in-memory data storage, we will next see how to migrate the code sample as part of a microservice.

Using in-memory data storage with Jakarta EE and MicroProfile

Thanks to the engines in the MicroProfile and Jakarta EE specifications, we can very easily choose which one best fits the application's goal. In *Chapter 5*, we discussed both specifications and why they are essential for the Java community:

1. To get started, you can access the MicroProfile website (`https://start.microprofile.io/`) and the starter project. It works just like the Spring initializer, for Spring-based applications.

2. Once on the page, confirm that MicroProfile version 3.3 is available, and choose one of the options. Make sure to check the **Config** checkbox in order to save some time and get some auto-generated basic files.

3. For this example, we'll use the **Helidon** runtime.

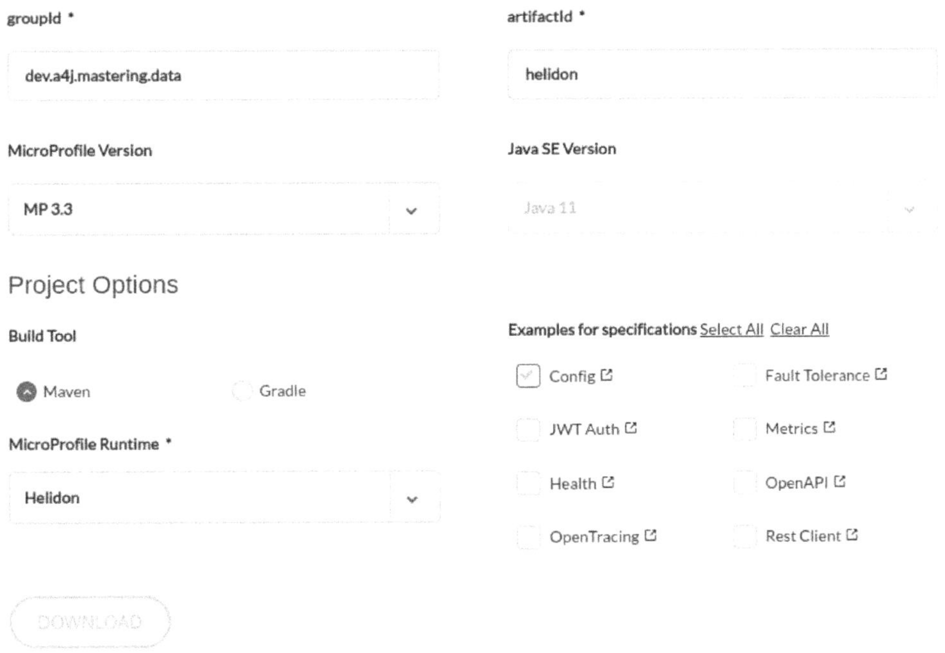

Figure 8.3 – MicroProfile starter website

4. Next, all we must do is add the Eclipse Store dependency to the pom.xml application, as the Eclipse MicroProfile implementation already provides both **config** and CDI:

```
<dependency>
    <groupId>one.microstream</groupId>
    <artifactId>eclipse-store-integrations-cdi
</artifactId>
    <version>07.00.00-MS-GA</version>
</dependency>
```

5. Next, use the ancient programmer technique… copy and paste! You can copy the dependency configurations from the previous project into your new MicroProfile-based project.

    Now, we need to be able to modify an entity, such as the Car entity. As the entity is immutable, creating new instances must be done through its constructor. The adoption of this good practice is not required by the data storage solution, Eclipse Store, but it is a good approach for using the entities in the REST endpoints.

    In the Car class, identify and annotate its constructor method with @JsonCreator and @JsonProperty, which come from the JSON binding specifications (https://jakarta.ee/specifications/jsonb/2.0/). Notice that these are not annotations required by Eclipse Store.

6. Change the Year type to Integer, to avoid creating a custom interface to serialize and deserialize data:

```
public class Car {

    private final String plate;
    private final Integer year;

    private final String make;

    private final String model;

    @JsonbCreator
    public Car(@JsonbProperty("plate") String plate,
              @JsonbProperty("year") Integer year,
              @JsonbProperty("make") String make,
              @JsonbProperty("model") String model) {
        this.plate = plate;
        this.year = year;
        this.make = make;
        this.model = model;
    }
}
```

We are building the `Car` entity as an immutable class; therefore, its fields are final and can be set by using injections on the constructor method. To help us achieve this goal, we'll use a JSONB-compatible implementation.

7. Add the `@JsonbCreator` annotation, to turn this class into an eligible bean for the API, and so that the `@JsonProperty` annotation can link the respective parameter with the defined JSON property.

> *Note*
>
> We can delete CarBuilder once the creation process is through JSON.

We'll create a resource where we'll see the path and URL. We'll expose all the services we made using the URL, so we'll have to list the cars by finding a model and inserting a car:

```
@ApplicationScoped
@Path("garage")
public class GarageResource {

    @Inject
    private CarService service;
    @GET
    public List<Car> getCars() {
        return this.service.getCars();
    }


    @Path("{model}")
    @GET
    public Car findByModel(@PathParam("model") String
      model) {
        return this.service.findByModel(model)
                .orElseThrow(() -> new
                    WebApplicationException(NOT_FOUND));
    }

    @POST
    public Car add(Car car) {
        this.service.add(car);
        return car;
    }
}
```

Our resource class is ready to be used on our microservices. As you can see here, we're injecting `CarService` and using this integration to connect with this `GarageResource`, which we can explore through HTTP requests.

We have all the code ready; let's build and execute the application:

```
mvn clean package
java -jar target/garage.jar
```

When the service is up, we can explore it by creating a frontend that consumes this service or using an HTTP client UI. We'll run our sample using `curl`. We'll make three cars and then return them from the service:

```
curl --location --request POST 'http://localhost:8080/garage' \
--header 'Content-Type: application/json' \
--data-raw '{"make": "Dodge", "model": "Wagon", "year": 1993, "plate":
"JN8AE2KP7D9956349"}'

curl --location --request POST 'http://localhost:8080/garage' \
--header 'Content-Type: application/json' \
--data-raw '{"make": "Ford", "model": "F250", "year": 2005, "plate":
"WBANE73577B200053"}'

curl --location --request POST 'http://localhost:8080/garage' \
--header 'Content-Type: application/json' \
--data-raw '{"make": "Honda", "model": "S2000", "year": 2005, "plate":
"WBANE73577B200053"}'

curl --location --request POST 'http://localhost:8080/garage' \
--header 'Content-Type: application/json' \
--data-raw '{"make": "Toyota", "model": "Corolla", "year": 2005,
"plate": "WBANE73577B200053"}'


curl --location --request GET 'http://localhost:8080/garage/Corolla'

curl --location --request GET 'http://localhost:8080/garage'
```

This was a sample HTTP request using the curl program; feel free to use any HTTP client that you wish, such as Postman.

We also need to append the Eclipse Store settings in this application. Another point is we updated the `ApplicationPath` annotation to `"/"`. Furthermore, we added the `Garage` resources, but we won't put the full details here; please, check out the repository to get all the details.

Summary

Eclipse Store brings a new persistence perspective; you can increase performance by reducing the mapper process. It impacts not only the application's response time but also cloud costs since it requires fewer machines, and consequently reduces infrastructure cost.

This chapter looked at Java integration with CDI on Java SE and microservices using MicroProfile. We saw the power of several databases and persistence solutions, but how can we merge them? You'll find out in the next chapter, about polyglot persistence.

Part 3:
Architectural Perspective over Persistence

In this section of the book, we take an architectural perspective on persistence, exploring various topics related to designing and implementing robust and scalable persistence solutions. This session delves into the architectural considerations and challenges associated with persistence in modern Java solutions, from polyglot persistence to modernization strategies.

This part has the following chapters:

- *Chapter 9, Persistence Practices: Exploring Polyglot Persistence*
- *Chapter 10, Architecting Distributed Systems: Challenges and Anti-Patterns*
- *Chapter 11, Modernization Strategies and Data Integration*
- *Chapter 12, Final Considerations on Persistence in Modern Java Solutions*

Persistence Practices – Exploring Polyglot Persistence

Software development has become more complex, requiring way more integration, and we need to innovate simultaneously to make our lives easier. One good option is to take advantage of several databases with polyglot persistence.

When we talk about persistence solutions, there are around 400, with different types, structures, and particular behavior that make sense in specific cases. The philosophy of polyglot persistence is to use the tool to find the right solution.

This chapter will introduce the principle of polyglot persistence and how to use it with Java.

We will discuss the following topics:

- The trade-offs of polyglot persistence
- Understanding **Domain-Driven Design (DDD)** and Jakarta
- Jakarta Data

Technical requirements

The following are the technical requirements for the chapter:

- Java 17
- Git
- Maven
- Any preferred IDE

The source code for the chapter is available at https://github.com/PacktPublishing/Persistence-Best-Practices-for-Java-Applications/tree/main/chapter-09.

The trade-offs of polyglot persistence

Polyglot persistence is an approach to data storage in which multiple types of databases are used together to address different needs within an application. The term **polyglot** refers to the use of various languages or tools, and in this context, it refers to the use of multiple types of databases.

In traditional monolithic applications, a single database is typically used to store all data types. However, this approach can become less effective as applications become more complex. Polyglot persistence, however, allows developers to choose the best database for each use case based on factors such as scalability, data structure, and query requirements.

For example, a social media platform might use a document database such as MongoDB to store user profiles and activity feeds, a graph database such as Neo4j to analyze social connections, and a relational database such as MySQL to manage transactions and payments.

By leveraging multiple databases, polyglot persistence can help improve an application's performance, scalability, and flexibility. However, it also comes with additional complexity in managing data consistency, migrations, and backups across multiple systems.

The idea of polyglots is always good and provides several opportunities for an application. The core idea is sound: taking advantage of a database in the perfect scenario is terrific. But, even with polyglot persistence, there are trade-offs, as with any software architecture decision.

More databases also mean greater cost and infrastructure knowledge to handle specific persistence solutions. Please be aware of this.

In Java, more databases mean more dependencies in the application, which might *add to the jar-hell headache*. The microservices approach will help you in this situation, *where each database in your environment has its own interface*; it also helps to isolate the technology from the business.

From a code design perspective, there is the Ports and Adapters pattern, or the Hexagonal model, where you can isolate the core logic of an application from the persistence layer. However, as mentioned, more layers mean more code overall, which means concerns about maintainability and bugs.

Starting simply with three layers, as in the **Model-View-Controller** (**MVC**) architectural pattern, and isolating them is a good start, such as beginning with a monolith instead of microservices. When the need arises, go for it and refactor the code.

Sometimes, we only need some of these layers for our applications; starting with enough architecture is an excellent way to manage risk in your architecture.

Recognizing the abstraction from/to the business layer and avoiding coupling it with the persistence layer as much as possible is crucial to an evolutionary architecture.

Common sense and pragmatism are the best formulas to define the best pattern for each scenario. As advice, think of software as a long-term project; we don't need to design a sophisticated Netflix-style architecture on the first day.

Based on the best practices, enjoying, taking advantage of, and exploring databases to take advantage of your system is possible. In the following figure, based on James Serra's article *What is Polyglot Persistence?* (https://www.jamesserra.com/archive/2015/07/what-is-polyglot-persistence/), you can get more context for which database is best suited to or a good candidate for a given scenario. It describes what type of database is recommended to address recurrent and key requirements of the listed use cases:

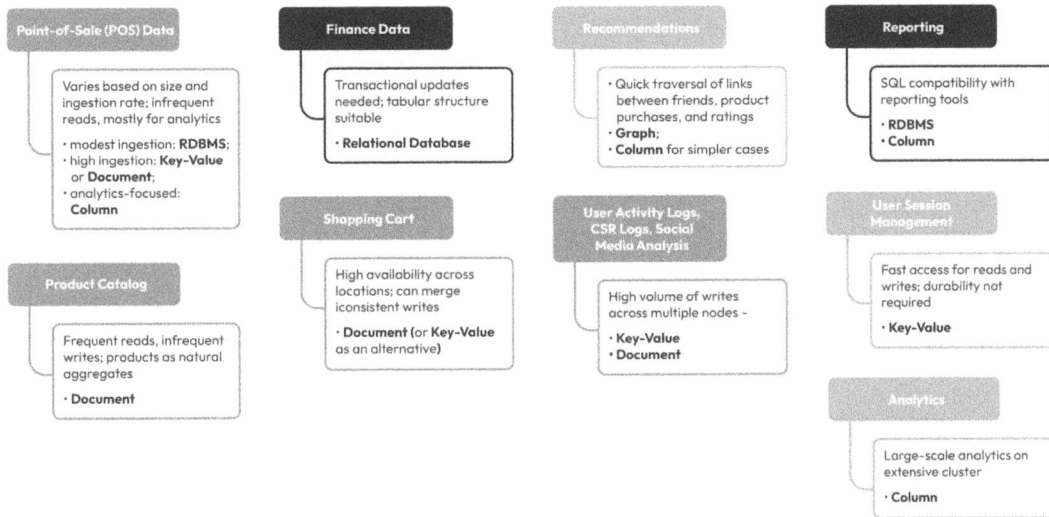

Figure 9.1 – Use cases and database types

Those are some possibilities of database uses based on the type; when we talk about NoSQL, remember that in some classes, there is particular behavior that makes sense and is worth using.

For long-term applications, migration is possible. The isolation can help you in the polyglot journey. The following section will introduce **DDD**, its impacts on the persistence layer, and how Jakarta can help us on this journey.

Understanding DDD and Jakarta

DDD is an approach to software development that focuses on understanding the problem domain and modeling it in code. DDD is based on the idea that the problem domain should be the primary focus of development and that the software should be designed to reflect the underlying domain concepts and processes.

DDD distinguishes between strategic and tactical design. Strategic design refers to the overall architecture and organization of the software, while tactical design refers to the detailed design of individual components and modules.

In strategic design, DDD emphasizes the importance of defining a clear and consistent domain model that represents the business concepts and processes in the problem domain. This model should be independent of any particular technology or implementation and should be based on a deep understanding of the domain. Strategic design also involves defining bounded contexts and specific domain areas with well-defined boundaries modeled separately from other parts of the domain.

Tactical design, on the other hand, focuses on the details of how individual components and modules are designed and implemented. DDD uses patterns and techniques such as aggregates, entities, value objects, and repositories to model and manipulate the domain objects in the tactical design.

DDD can significantly impact the different layers of a software application, including the presentation layer, application layer, domain layer, and persistence layer. Here's a brief overview of how DDD can apply to and impact each layer:

- **The presentation layer**: DDD can impact the presentation layer by providing a clear and consistent domain model that can be used to guide the design of user interfaces and user interactions. The presentation layer should reflect the domain model. It should provide a user-friendly interface that enables users to interact with the application in a way that makes sense from a domain perspective.

- **The application layer**: DDD can impact the application layer by providing a clear and consistent set of services and operations that reflects the business processes and workflows in the domain. The application layer should be designed to support the domain model and should provide a layer of abstraction, which enables the domain layer to focus on business logic rather than implementation details.

- **The domain layer**: DDD has the most significant impact on the domain layer, which is the heart of the application. In the domain layer, DDD emphasizes the importance of modeling the domain using a rich and expressive language that reflects the business concepts and processes. The domain layer should be designed to be independent of any specific technology or implementation and focused on encapsulating business logic and domain knowledge.

- **The persistence layer**: DDD can also impact the persistence layer by providing a clear and consistent way of mapping domain objects to the database. DDD emphasizes repositories, which provide a layer of abstraction between the domain layer and the persistence layer. Repositories enable the domain layer to focus on business logic rather than database access and provide a way to ensure that domain objects are persisted and retrieved consistently and reliably.

Overall, DDD can significantly impact the design and architecture of a software application and can help ensure that the application is focused on the problem domain rather than implementation details. DDD can help create more maintainable and scalable software that is adaptable to changing business requirements by providing a clear and consistent domain model and a set of design patterns and techniques.

The repository pattern is a design pattern that provides a layer of abstraction between the domain layer and the persistence layer. The repository pattern encapsulates the logic for accessing and persisting domain objects. It provides a way to ensure that domain objects are stored and retrieved consistently and reliably.

Using repositories, the domain layer can be designed to be independent of the persistence layer. It can be focused on modeling business processes and workflows using rich and expressive language. The repository pattern can significantly impact the persistence layer by enabling the domain layer to focus on business logic and domain knowledge rather than implementation details such as database access and querying.

The repository pattern is typically implemented as an interface in the domain layer, with a concrete implementation in the persistence layer. The repository interface defines a set of methods for storing, retrieving, and querying domain objects. The concrete implementation provides the actual implementation of these methods using the persistence technology of choice (such as a relational or NoSQL database).

One of the key benefits of the repository pattern is that it enables the domain layer to be decoupled from the persistence layer, making the application more modular and easier to maintain. By separating concerns and encapsulating logic, the repository pattern can ensure that the application is more flexible and adaptable to changing requirements.

The repository pattern is often compared to the **Data Access Object (DAO)** pattern, another design pattern for accessing and persisting data. The main difference between a repository and a DAO is a repository is designed to encapsulate the logic for accessing and persisting domain objects. In contrast, a DAO is designed to encapsulate general logic for accessing and persisting data. The following figure shows the sequence starting from the controller to the database and returning to the controller.

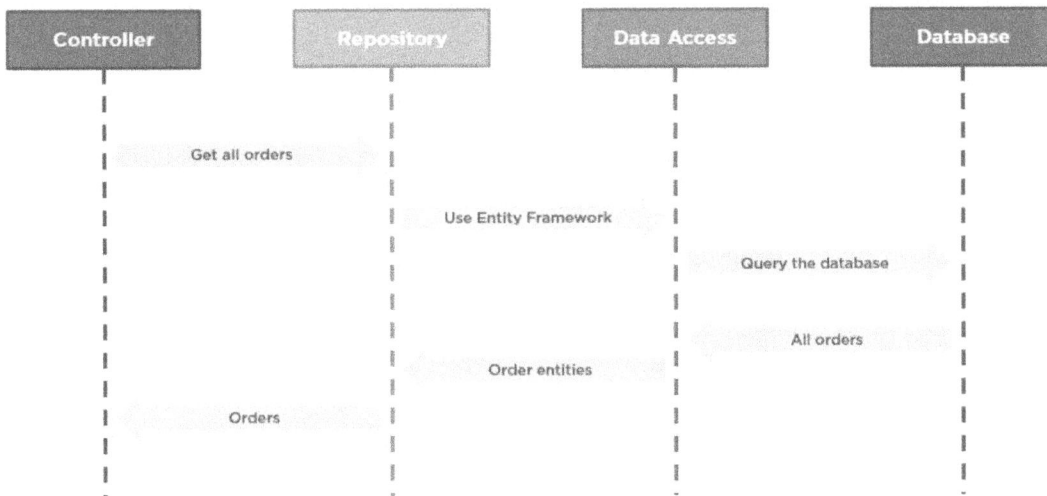

Figure 9.2 – Sequence from the controller to the database

In other words, a DAO is typically focused on low-level details, such as database connections, transactions, and SQL statements. In contrast, a repository focuses on the domain model's higher-level concerns. While both patterns can be used for persistence, the repository pattern is often considered more aligned with the principles of DDD, as it provides a way to ensure that the persistence layer is designed to support the domain model and business logic.

Where does the data come from? We don't need to know the source of the database, whether it comes from SQL, NoSQL, or a web service. The client does need to know.

The following figure shows this idea, where we have the business layer injecting a persistence layer, and it does matter where the data source comes from; it might be coming from all of the sources simultaneously.

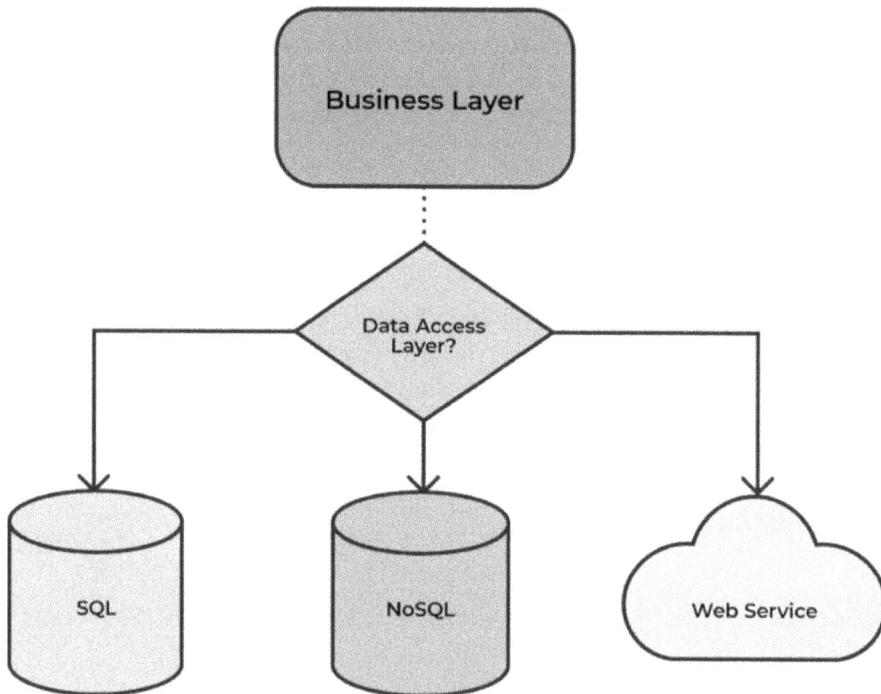

Figure 9.3 – A DDD repository representation

Let's see some code to explore the capabilities of Jakarta Data in the first version that released the repository feature. As with MicroStream, we'll start with Java SE and then move the application to Jakarta EE. We'll create two CRUD operations using both the `Developer` and `Airplane` entities, where the second will handle simple pagination code.

Jakarta Data

Designing an application with multiple database systems is one of the hardest things to do in the software world. Fortunately, there is a specification that makes it easier to implement polyglot persistence in Java. It is a persistence-agnostic API that connects to different types of databases and storage sources seamlessly. The API offered by Jakarta Data enables convenient access to data technologies, making it possible for Java developers to divide their persistence and model concerns into distinct features. For instance, a repository interface can be created with a query method that the framework will implement.

Exploring agnostic design patterns is one of the goals of Jakarta Data; the first feature of this specification is the DDD repository pattern. The objective of the repository is to facilitate polyglot persistence without impacting the business.

Starting with dependencies, from now on, we'll add only the API; then, we'll start to explain the implementations. So, we'll include the Jakarta Data dependency:

```
<dependency>
    <groupId>jakarta.data</groupId>
    <artifactId>jakarta-data-api</artifactId>
    <version>${data.version}</version>
</dependency>
```

We will create both the `Developer` and `Airline` entities. In the Jakarta Data API, we must define the entity and its IDs using `@Entity` and `@Id`, respectively. Hey, how about adding other fields? It varies with the implementation; for example, in JPA, this is enough, whereas in Jakarta NoSQL, we need to identify the other fields with the `@Column` annotation:

```
@Entity
public class Developer {

    @Id
    private String nickname;
    private String name;
    private String city;
    private String language;
}


@Entity
public class Airplane {
```

```
    @Id
    private String model;
    private String manufacturer;
    private String nationality;
    private int seats;
}
```

We have the entities; the next step is the persistence layer with a repository. Once we have two different entities, we'll create two separate repositories.

This interface provides several methods the user doesn't need to implement; the vendor will implement them. The first one relates to the `Developer` entity and uses the most basic repository: `CrudDataRepository`. Furthermore, there is the method that uses querying, where you can, using the convention, create queries that you don't need to implement; the vendor will implement them.

`DeveloperRepository` is the Developer repository, an interface that extends `CrudDataRepository`. Now we will go through several methods; furthermore, we will create a query to find by language using the `findByLanguage` method:

```
@Repository
public interface DeveloperRepository extends
  CrudRepository<Developer, String> {

    List<Developer> findByLanguage(String language);
}
```

The next step is the `Airplane` repository, so we have our `Hangar`, but wait!? Should it be `AirplaneRepository` instead? We have a convention of using the `Repository` suffix. However, you can use the collection of the entity, such as `Garage` for a collection of cars or `Team` for a collection of players.

The `Hangar` interface extends a different interface, this time, `PageableRepository`. It is a specialization that enables pagination resources. It uses the query method and returns a `Page` interface to work with a slice of information on airplanes:

```
@Repository
public interface Hangar extends
  PageableRepository<Airplane, String> {

    Page<Hangar> findByManufacturer(String manufacturer,
      Pageable pageable);
}
```

Finally, we have both code repositories ready for execution. Starting with the `Developer` repository, we'll create developers, find them by ID, delete them by ID, and use the method we made, which is querying by language:

```
public class App {

    public static void main(String[] args) {
        try (SeContainer container =
            SeContainerInitializer.newInstance().initialize()) {

            DeveloperRepository repository = container
                .select(DeveloperRepository.class).get();

            Developer otavio = Developer.builder()
                    .name("Otavio Santana")
                    .city("Salvador")
                    .nickname("ptavopkava")
                    .language("Java")
                    .build();

            Developer kvarel4 = Developer.builder()
                    .name("Karina Varela")
                    .city("Brasília")
                    .nickname("kvarel4")
                    .language("Java")
                    .build();

            repository.save(otavio);
            repository.save(kvarel4);
            Optional<Developer> developer = repository
                .findById(otavio.getNickname());
            List<Developer> java = repository
                .findByLanguage("Java");
            System.out.println("Java developers: " + java);
            repository.delete(otavio);
        }
    }
}
```

The next step is to execute the pagination resource with pagination in our Hangar. Once we have a few airplanes added, we'll include pagination with a size of two elements. In the real world, the number is more considerable. It will vary based on the area and context; it is often between 10 and 100:

```
try (SeContainer container =
    SeContainerInitializer.newInstance().initialize()) {
```

```java
Hangar hangar = container
  .select(Hangar.class).get();

Airplane freighters = Airplane.builder()
 .model("Freighters")
        .manufacturer("Boeing")
        .nationality("United States")
        .seats(149)
        .build();

Airplane max = Airplane.builder().model("Max")
        .manufacturer("Boeing").nationality("United
        States")
        .seats(149)
        .build();

Airplane nextGeneration = Airplane.builder()
        .model("Next-Generation 737")
        .manufacturer("Boeing").nationality("United
        States")
        .seats(149)
        .build();

Airplane dreamliner = Airplane.builder()
        .model("Dreamliner")
        .manufacturer("Boeing").nationality("United
        States")
        .seats(248)
        .build();

hangar.saveAll(List.of(freighters, max,
  nextGeneration));

Pageable pageable = Pageable.ofSize(1)
        .sortBy(Sort.asc("manufacturer"));

Page<Airplane> page = hangar.findAll(pageable);

System.out.println("The first page: " +
  page.content());

Pageable nextPageable = page.nextPageable();
```

```
    Page<Airplane> page2 =
      hangar.findAll(nextPageable);

    System.out.println("The second page: " +
      page2.content());


}
```

We have both running on Java SE; let's move on to the next stage, which is pushing the same code to `MicroProfile` to create a microservice. In the chapter about `MicroStream` in *Chapter 8*, we explained the CDI engine/core; we'll follow the same principle – copy/paste the same code and change the access to make it a rest resource instead of a Java SE application:

```
@ApplicationScoped
@Consumes(MediaType.APPLICATION_JSON)
@Produces(MediaType.APPLICATION_JSON)
@Path("developers")
public class DeveloperResource {


    private final DeveloperRepository repository;

    @Inject
    public DeveloperResource(DeveloperRepository
     repository) {
        this.repository = repository;
    }

    @GET
    public List<Developer> getDevelopers() {
        return this.repository.findAll()
          .collect(Collectors.toUnmodifiableList());
    }

    @GET
    @Path("{id}")
    public Developer findById(@PathParam("id") String id) {
        return this.repository.findById(id)
        .orElseThrow(() -> new WebApplicationException
          (Response.Status.NOT_FOUND));
    }

    @PUT
```

```
public Developer insert(Developer developer) {
    return this.repository.save(developer);
}


@DELETE
@Path("{id}")
public void deleteById(@PathParam("id") String id) {
    this.repository.deleteById(id);
}


}
```

We showed the pure API, but how about the implementations? To display the number of options, we have a repository that illustrates an implementation of the particular behavior to each example in our git remote. You can try out, run, and get a feel for the difference between vendors and persistence solutions.

Summary

Polyglot persistence is a good path to advance most enterprise applications. It is possible to explore SQL, NoSQL, or any persistence solution with this approach. However, as with any architectural decision, pay attention to the trade-offs; an abstraction can ensure that the choice of database will not impact the business perspective.

Jakarta Data helps standardize behavior and code patterns. It helps us build a universe of capabilities out of several persistence solutions. It is promising solution to increase the capabilities around data persistence patterns on Java, and it is open for help and feedback; join us to make our lives even easier when working with this tool.

It's now time to explore, at an architectural level, the integration practices that allow us to explore the best out-of-data integration patterns in modern cloud-oriented solutions.

10
Architecting Distributed Systems – Challenges and Anti-Patterns

In today's digital landscape, the demand for scalable and reliable systems has led to the widespread adoption of distributed systems. These complex networks of interconnected components are designed to handle large-scale data processing, storage, and communication across multiple machines or nodes. However, architecting distributed systems comes with a unique set of challenges and pitfalls.

Building distributed systems aims to achieve high availability, fault tolerance, and better performance and scalability while distributing the workload across multiple nodes. However, the complexity of these systems often gives rise to various challenges that architects and developers must overcome. From ensuring data consistency and synchronization to managing network latency and optimizing performance, numerous factors should be considered when designing a distributed system.

One of the critical challenges in architecting distributed systems is achieving proper data consistency. Maintaining the integrity and coherence of data across different nodes is crucial, but it becomes increasingly challenging as the system scales. Ensuring that all replicas of a given piece of data are updated correctly and simultaneously poses a significant challenge and often requires implementing complex synchronization mechanisms.

Another challenge lies in managing network latency and communication overhead. In a distributed system, nodes communicate with each other over a network, and the time taken for messages to traverse the network can introduce delays and bottlenecks. Architects must carefully design communication protocols and choose appropriate network technologies to minimize latency and maximize system performance.

Scalability is a critical consideration when architecting distributed systems. As the demand for resources and processing power grows, the system should scale horizontally by adding more nodes seamlessly. Achieving this scalability while maintaining performance and avoiding bottlenecks is a complex task that requires careful planning and architectural decisions.

Despite these challenges, architects must also be aware of common anti-patterns that can undermine the effectiveness and reliability of distributed systems. Anti-patterns are recurring design or implementation practices that are considered suboptimal or counterproductive. These can include network congestion, single points of failure, improper load balancing, or overreliance on a central coordinator. Recognizing and avoiding these anti-patterns is crucial to ensuring the successful operation of distributed systems.

In this chapter, we will explore the pitfalls of modern architecture when we talk about distributed systems:

- Data integration scales and distributed transactions
- The dual-write anti-pattern
- Microservices and shared databases
- Eventual consistency problems

We will delve into the challenges architects face when designing distributed systems and explore common anti-patterns that can arise during the process. By understanding these challenges and avoiding the pitfalls, architects and developers can create robust and efficient distributed systems that meet the demands of modern applications. Through best practices and practical insights, we aim to equip you with the knowledge and tools to architect distributed systems and mitigate potential risks effectively.

Data integration scales and distributed transactions

Data integration is critical to building distributed systems, where disparate data sources must be harmonized and accessible to various system components. As the scale of data and the number of distributed nodes increase, the challenges associated with data integration becomes more challenging. One key consideration in this context is the coordination of distributed transactions.

Maintaining data integrity is crucial for distributed transactions and ensuring that the system behaves as if it's executing a single transaction on a centralized database. Distributed transactions refer to related database operations that must be executed atomically across multiple nodes. In a distributed system, where data is spread across different nodes, ensuring consistency and isolation across these operations becomes complex.

The following figure shows data being integrated into two services, each with a database. At this point, orchestration is required to guarantee data consistency and security:

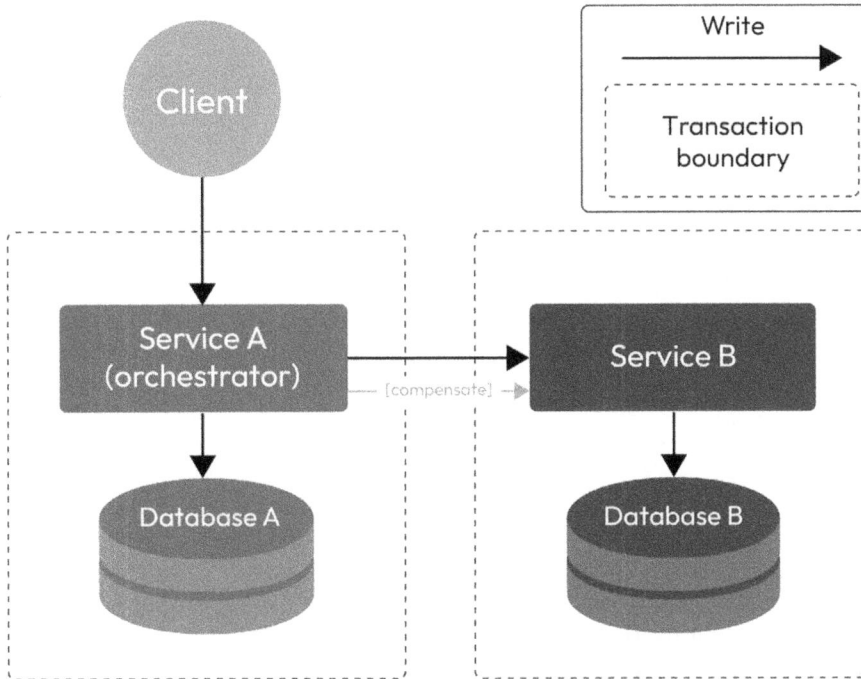

Figure 10.1: Transaction workflow in a distributed system

However, achieving distributed transactional consistency at scale poses significant challenges. Traditional **atomicity, consistency, isolation, and durability** (**ACID**) properties, typically guaranteed in a centralized database, become harder to enforce across distributed nodes due to network latency, node failures, and concurrency issues.

One approach to addressing these challenges is to use distributed transaction protocols such as **two-phase commit** (**2PC**) or **three-phase commit** (**3PC**). These protocols coordinate the commit or rollback decisions across multiple nodes in a distributed transaction. However, these protocols have limitations, including increased latency and failure vulnerability if a coordinator node becomes unavailable. The following diagram shows a sequence of 2PCs:

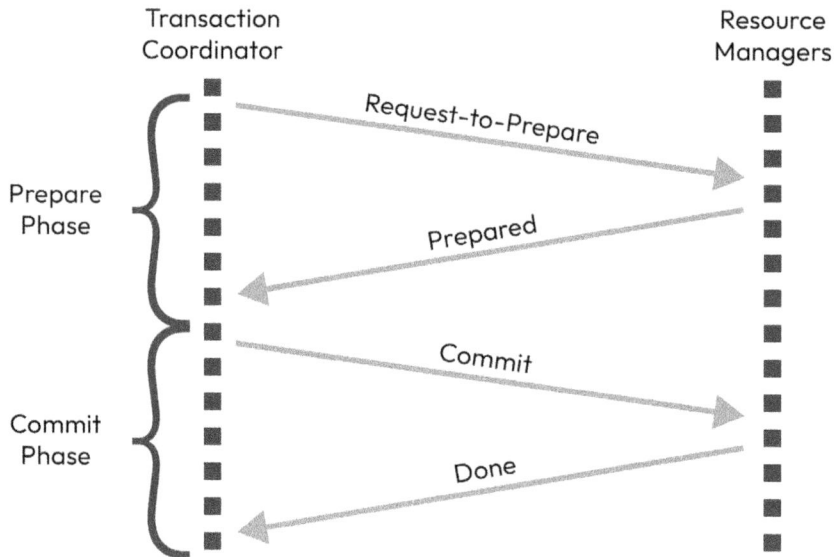

Figure 10.2: 2PC illustration

Another approach is to adopt a more relaxed consistency model, such as eventual consistency or optimistic concurrency control. These models trade off strict consistency guarantees for increased scalability and availability. These models can perform better when real-time consistency is not strictly required by allowing temporary inconsistencies and resolving conflicts asynchronously.

Furthermore, distributed data integration often involves dealing with heterogeneous data sources with varying schemas and formats. Data transformation and mapping become crucial to ensure that data from different sources can be effectively combined and processed and often come with a performance cost. To create a consistent view of a distributed system, you can use methods such as **extract**, **transform**, and **load** (**ETL**) or data virtualization to combine data from various sources.

Distributed transactional systems require careful design decisions to balance the trade-offs between consistency, scalability, and performance. When designing and architecting data integration at scale, it is essential to consider data consistency requirements, latency, fault tolerance, and performance factors. Understanding the characteristics and limitations of different transactional models and adopting appropriate data integration techniques can help architects and developers tackle the complexities associated with distributed data integration and ensure the reliability and efficiency of their systems.

In summary, data integration at scale in distributed systems requires addressing the challenges of distributed transactions and maintaining consistency across multiple nodes. Architects and developers must consider the trade-offs between consistency guarantees, scalability, and performance when designing distributed transactional systems. Organizations can effectively manage and integrate large-scale data into their distributed systems by employing appropriate transactional protocols, consistency models, and data integration techniques.

Distributed databases are challenging, so we should leverage the best architecture to minimize pitfalls. Next, we'll discuss an error that's recorded when managing a distrusted system that's specifically related to the dual-write process and why it should be avoided.

The dual-write anti-pattern

Dual-write is a pattern or approach in software development where data is simultaneously written to two or more separate systems or databases in real time. Dual-write aims to ensure data consistency and synchronization across multiple systems that serve different purposes or require additional data. The following diagram shows this operation, where a single web app writes multiple times to a database, a cache, and a second application.

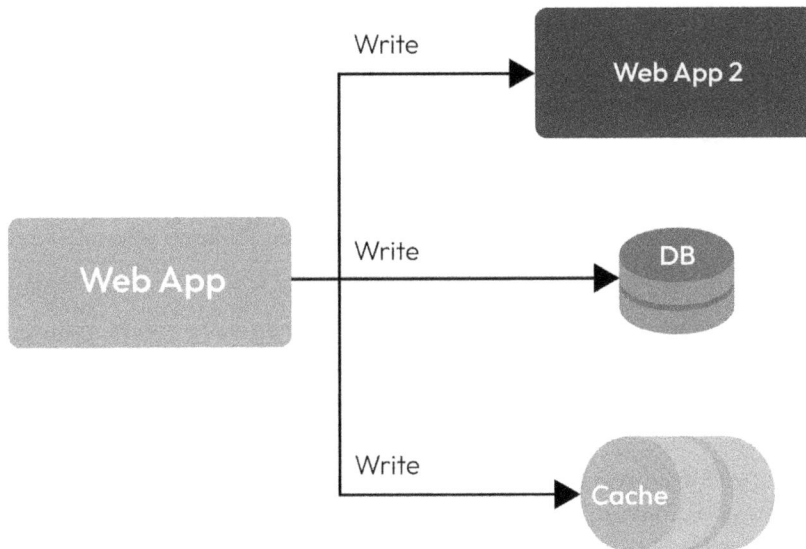

Figure 10.3: Dual-write operation

While dual-write may seem convenient for data integration and synchronization, it is generally considered an anti-pattern. But what happens if one update succeeds and the other fails? Here are a few reasons why dual-write can be problematic:

- **Complexity and coupling**: Implementing dual-write introduces complexity and tight coupling between different systems. It increases the maintenance overhead and makes the system more fragile and prone to errors. Any change or update in one system may require corresponding changes in all the other systems involved in the dual-write process.

- **Performance overhead**: Dual-write can have a significant performance impact on the system. Writing data to multiple systems synchronously in real time can introduce latency and decrease the overall system performance. As the number of systems involved increases, the impact on performance becomes more pronounced, potentially leading to a degraded user experience.

- **Inconsistencies and failures**: Dual-write does not guarantee perfect consistency across all systems. Failures during writing, such as network issues or system failures, can lead to inconsistent data states across different systems. Handling these failures and resolving inconsistencies can be challenging and time-consuming.

- **Data integrity challenges**: Maintaining data integrity becomes more complex with dual-write. Ensuring that all the systems involved are updated correctly and simultaneously, without any data loss or corruption, requires implementing sophisticated mechanisms such as distributed transactions. These mechanisms add complexity and can further impact performance.

- **Scalability limitations**: Dual-write becomes increasingly challenging to scale as the system grows. As the number of designs and the volume of data increase, the overhead of synchronizing writes across all systems becomes more challenging to manage effectively. Scaling dual-write to handle high-throughput scenarios may require additional infrastructure and optimization efforts.

Instead of depending solely on dual-write, let's explore other options for integrating and synchronizing data. Some recommended alternatives include the following:

- **ETL**: Using ETL processes, data can be extracted from the source system, transformed into the appropriate format, and then loaded into the target system. This approach allows for more flexibility and decoupling between systems, enabling data transformations and mappings as necessary.

- **Event-driven architecture**: Employing an event-driven architecture can help propagate data changes or events across systems asynchronously. It decouples systems and allows for more flexible and scalable data integration. Events are published when data changes occur, and interested systems that are subscribed, can react to these events accordingly.

- **Message queues**: Leveraging message queues can provide reliable and scalable data integration and synchronization mechanisms. Systems can publish messages to the queue, and subscribing systems can consume them at their own pace, ensuring asynchronous and decoupled communication.

Organizations can achieve data integration and synchronization by adopting these alternative approaches while avoiding dual-write pitfalls. These approaches provide more flexibility, scalability, and maintainability, enabling better-distributed data system management.

Unfortunately, dual-write is the most popular anti-pattern we face as distributed architects and is a mistake. Now, let's move to the second topic: microservices and shared databases.

Microservices and shared databases

The use of microservices architecture has become increasingly popular because it allows you to create scalable and flexible systems. This approach involves breaking down applications into smaller, independent services that can be developed, deployed, and scaled individually. However, despite its many advantages, sharing databases across multiple services can pose challenges and disadvantages.

The following figure illustrates a sample where three applications share the same database. In the short term, we can imagine that this will save us some power resources, but in the long term, we start wondering about the price. If we create an inconsistent data event, how do we know which application contains the bug? We may also have security issues, such as unauthorized data access:

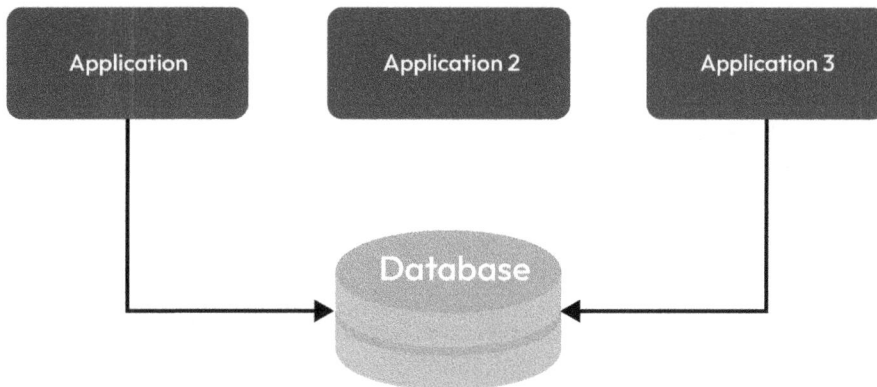

Figure 10.4: Shared database in a microservice

Multiple microservices sharing a database can introduce several challenges and drawbacks. These include data coupling and dependencies, performance bottlenecks, lack of autonomy and ownership, data integrity and consistency issues, and scalability and deployment flexibility limitations. The tight coupling between services due to shared data can slow development and hinder individual service flexibility. Contentions for database resources can lead to degraded performance, especially when multiple services concurrently access the same database. Shared databases also blur the lines of ownership and make it harder to identify responsible services for data-related issues. Ensuring data integrity and consistency becomes complex with multiple services writing to the same database, and conflicts and inconsistencies may arise. Scaling the database to accommodate the load from numerous services becomes challenging, and deploying new services or making changes can be complicated due to necessary schema changes and migrations affecting other services.

- **Data coupling and dependencies**: Sharing a database between multiple microservices introduces tight coupling between services. Database schema or data model changes can impact multiple services, requiring coordination and synchronization efforts. It can slow development and hinder individual services' flexibility and autonomy.

- **Performance bottlenecks:** When multiple services access the same shared database, contention for database resources can become a bottleneck. Increased traffic and simultaneous requests from various services can lead to degraded performance since the database becomes a single point of contention. Scaling the database becomes more challenging as the load from multiple services must be accommodated.

- **Lack of autonomy and ownership:** Microservices architecture emphasizes the autonomy and ownership of individual services. Sharing a database blurs the lines of ownership as multiple services have access to and can modify the same data. It can create confusion and make identifying the responsible service for data-related issues or errors easier.

- **Data integrity and consistency:** Maintaining data integrity becomes more complex when multiple services are written to the same database. Coordinating transactions and managing concurrency becomes more complex when multiple services are involved. Ensuring consistency and enforcing business rules across services can be challenging as conflicts and data inconsistencies may arise.

- **Scalability and deployment flexibility:** Shared databases can limit microservices' scalability and deployment flexibility. As the system grows, scaling the database becomes more challenging due to the increased load from multiple services. Additionally, deploying new services or changing existing services becomes more complicated as they may require database schema changes or data migrations that affect other services.

The following diagram shows the isolation between several services, where each service has a dedicated database and is responsible for it. All communication between applications will happen through an API; no application communicates directly with another application's database:

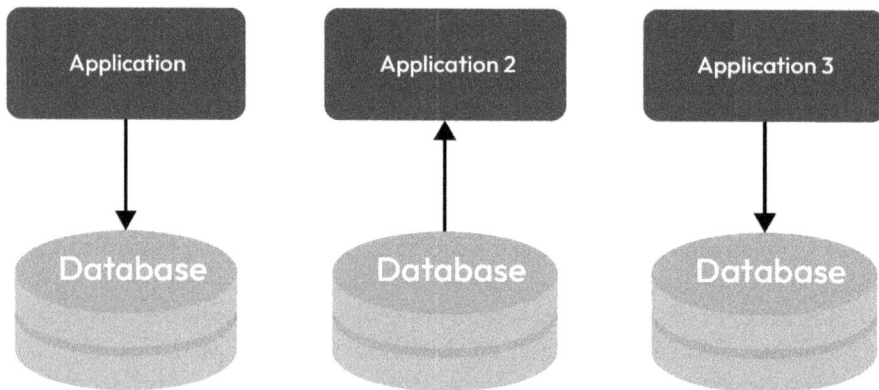

Figure 10.5: A microservice with each microservice has its own database

To tackle these obstacles, utilizing one database for each microservice is advisable. This approach offers numerous advantages, as follows:

- **Service autonomy and isolation**: Each microservice has a dedicated database, providing independence and isolation. Each service can choose the database technology or schema that best suits its needs. Services can evolve independently without them impacting others, allowing faster development, deployment, and scalability.

- **Simplified data management**: Data management becomes more straightforward with a single database per microservice. It reduces coordination efforts and allows services to choose the most suitable data storage technology or approach. Services fully control their data, including schema changes, migrations, and optimizations.

- **Improved performance and scalability**: Dedicated databases enable services to scale horizontally and independently. Services can choose databases optimized for their specific workload, ensuring efficient data access and processing. Each service can handle its database load, improving performance and scalability.

- **Clear ownership and responsibility**: Having single databases per microservice ensures a clear sense of ownership and responsibility. Each service is responsible for its data, making troubleshooting and resolving issues easier. Additionally, it enhances the system's maintainability and supportability.

- **Simplified data consistency and integrity**: Maintaining data consistency and integrity becomes more manageable with dedicated databases. Services can enforce their own business rules and transactional boundaries within their databases. It reduces the complexity of managing distributed transactions and mitigates data consistency issues.

Integration between services in a microservices architecture should ideally go through events, and it is generally considered a security best practice to avoid directly accessing or modifying another service's database. By relying on events for communication and maintaining strict boundaries around each service's database, you can enhance security and protect sensitive data within the system.

Here's why events and avoiding direct database access promote security:

- **Limited attack surface area**: Accessing another service's database increases the attack surface area. Exposing the database context of a service to other services introduces potential vulnerabilities, such as injection attacks or unauthorized access to sensitive data. Using events as a communication mechanism, you can limit the exposure of a service's data and reduce the risk of unauthorized access.

- **Data isolation**: Each service in a microservices architecture has its specific context and boundaries. By avoiding direct access to another service's database, you maintain data isolation and prevent unauthorized read or write operations on the database. This isolation ensures that only the service responsible for a specific data context can manipulate or access that data, enhancing security and data privacy.

- **Separation of concerns**: Microservices architecture emphasizes separation of concerns, where each service focuses on its specific domain. Allowing services to access each other's databases can blur these boundaries and introduce potential data inconsistencies or unauthorized modifications. By relying on events, services can communicate and exchange relevant data without breaking the encapsulation and ownership of their respective databases.

- **Auditing and compliance**: Maintaining separate database contexts for each service simplifies auditing and compliance requirements. With dedicated databases, tracking and monitoring data access and modifications within a specific service's context becomes easier. It supports compliance with regulatory standards and simplifies identifying and investigating security-related issues or breaches.

The **Saga design pattern** is used for long-running and distributed transactions. It allows a sequence of local transactions, each within the context of a specific service, to participate in a coordinated and consistent operation across multiple services. The Saga pattern enables communication and maintains data consistency across services without direct database access.

With the Saga pattern, each service involved in a transaction executes its part and emits an event to indicate the completion or progress of its task. Other services interested in the transaction listen to these events and continue their tasks accordingly. The Saga pattern ensures data consistency without directly exposing or modifying another service's database by relying on events and a coordinated sequence of local transactions.

By adopting the event-driven architecture and leveraging the Saga pattern, microservices can securely communicate and maintain data consistency while upholding the principles of isolation, limited surface area, and separation of concerns. This approach enhances security and minimizes the risks associated with direct access to other service databases, enabling a more robust and secure microservices ecosystem.

Using several good practices in distributed architecture can reduce the number of pitfalls and challenges but not eliminate them. It is a perennial challenge to get consistency across persistent systems. However, there is one point that we need to understand and live with: **eventual consistency**. In the next section, we'll discuss this in more detail.

Eventual consistency problems

In distributed systems, eventual consistency is a model where data updates are not instantly synchronized across all nodes. Instead, temporary inconsistencies are allowed, and the updates are gradually propagated until the system converges to a consistent state.

In eventual consistency, different nodes in the system may have different views of the data at any given point in time. This is primarily due to network latency, communication delays, and concurrent updates. However, eventual consistency ensures the system reaches a consistent state where all nodes converge on the same data.

To address the challenges and potential problems associated with eventual consistency, several techniques and mechanisms can be employed:

- **Conflicts** can occur when multiple updates are made to the same data simultaneously. To ensure consistency, conflict resolution mechanisms are used to determine how these conflicts should be resolved. Different techniques, including last-write-wins and application-defined conflict resolution strategies, can reconcile conflicting updates.

- **Read repair**: Read repair is a technique that's used to repair inconsistencies by updating or synchronizing data during read operations. When a read operation encounters inconsistent or outdated data, it triggers a repair process that retrieves the latest version of the data from other nodes and updates the local copy, ensuring eventual consistency.

- **Anti-entropy mechanisms**: Anti-entropy mechanisms actively detect and reconcile inconsistencies in distributed systems. These mechanisms periodically compare data across nodes and initiate synchronization processes to ensure consistency. Examples of anti-entropy tools include Merkle trees, gossip protocols, and vector clocks.

- **Quorum systems**: Quorum systems determine the level of agreement required to achieve consistency in a distributed system. By defining quorums and quorum sizes, systems can ensure that a certain number of nodes must agree on an update or operation before it is considered consistent. This helps prevent inconsistencies due to partial updates or failures.

- **Compensating actions**: In cases where conflicts or inconsistent updates cannot be resolved automatically, compensating actions can be employed. Compensating actions are operations or processes that reverse or pay for incorrect or conflicting updates. These actions help restore consistency in the system.

- **Idempotency**: Designing operations to be idempotent can help mitigate inconsistencies. Idempotence, in programming and mathematics, is a property of some operations such that no matter how many times you execute them, you achieve the same result. It ensures that even if an operation is used numerous times due to communication delays or retries, the outcome remains the same, preventing inconsistencies.

If you're familiar with NoSQL databases, you'll remember **BASE** means **basically available**, where data values may change over time but will achieve eventual consistency. This eventual consistency is the data modeling concept we must consider to meet several horizontal scalabilities, and we can take advantage of the knowledge we learn from the NoSQL database. We could see several previously mentioned techniques being used on this database engine, such as Cassandra as read-repair.

It's important to note that eventual consistency is unsuitable for all scenarios. Systems that require strict real-time consistency or those dealing with critical data may require more vital consistency models. However, for many distributed systems, eventual consistency strikes a balance between availability, performance, and data integrity.

Implementing and managing eventual consistency requires carefully considering the system's requirements, using appropriate conflict resolution strategies, and choosing anti-entropy mechanisms. By employing these techniques, distributed systems can effectively handle temporary inconsistencies and converge toward a consistent state over time.

Summary

In conclusion, architecting distributed systems presents unique challenges that must be carefully addressed to ensure the success and effectiveness of the system. Throughout this chapter, we explored some challenges, such as dual-write and microservices with shared databases, and discussed why they could be problematic.

Although initially appealing for data consistency, dual-write can introduce complexity, performance overhead, and data integrity challenges. Similarly, sharing databases between microservices can lead to data coupling, performance bottlenecks, and compromised autonomy. These pitfalls emphasize the importance of carefully considering alternatives, such as event-driven architectures and single databases per microservice, to promote scalability, independence, and maintainability.

We also highlighted the significance of eventual consistency as a model for distributed systems. While it allows temporary data inconsistencies, eventual consistency balances availability, performance, and data integrity. Techniques such as conflict resolution, read repair, anti-entropy mechanisms, quorum systems, compensating actions, and idempotency help address any challenges and ensure eventual consistency.

Furthermore, documentation emerges as a critical aspect of distributed architecture. Good documentation provides a comprehensive overview of the system, its components, and their interactions. It enables better understanding, collaboration, and decision-making throughout development, maintenance, and modernization.

The next chapter will delve into modernization strategies and data integration. We will explore approaches to modernizing existing systems, leverage data integration techniques, and delve into the various patterns and technologies that facilitate smooth transitions and effective utilization of distributed architectures.

11
Modernization Strategies and Data Integration

In today's fast-paced and data-driven world, businesses constantly strive to keep up with the evolving technology landscape. Modernization has become a key focus for organizations across industries, aiming to improve efficiency, agility, and competitiveness. One critical aspect of modernization is data integration, which plays a pivotal role in harnessing the power of data for informed decision-making. By adopting modernization strategies, avoiding anti-patterns, and leveraging modern cloud services, businesses can unlock the full potential of their data and gain a competitive edge in the market.

Modernization strategies encompass a range of approaches aimed at upgrading legacy systems, processes, and infrastructure to align with contemporary technological advancements. These strategies involve transforming traditional on-premises systems into cloud-based architectures, leveraging microservices and containers for increased scalability and agility, and adopting DevOps practices to streamline development and deployment processes. The ultimate goal is to modernize the entire IT landscape, ensuring it can keep pace with the demands of the digital era

However, modernization efforts can be challenging, and organizations must be mindful of potential anti-patterns that can hinder progress. Anti-patterns are common pitfalls or ineffective practices that can impede successful modernization initiatives. One notable anti-pattern is the lack of proper data integration, where siloed data sources and disparate systems hinder the ability to derive valuable insights. Businesses increasingly adopt **Change Data Capture** (**CDC**) techniques to overcome this challenge. CDC allows organizations to capture and propagate real-time data changes, enabling near-instantaneous updates and synchronization between different systems. By implementing CDC, organizations can ensure that their data integration efforts are efficient, accurate, and timely.

An anti-pattern is a recurring solution or approach that initially appears to be the correct way to solve a problem but ultimately leads to negative consequences or suboptimal outcomes.

Cloud computing has revolutionized the IT landscape, providing organizations with unprecedented scalability, flexibility, and cost-efficiency. Cloud-native technologies, such as serverless computing and containerization, enable organizations to build highly scalable and resilient applications that adapt to fluctuating workloads and evolving business needs. By migrating legacy systems to the cloud, businesses can take advantage of robust infrastructure, managed services, and advanced analytics capabilities offered by cloud providers. Furthermore, modernization strategies can significantly benefit from leveraging modern cloud services.

In this chapter, we'll explore more about those topics:

- Application modernization strategies
- Avoiding data storage-related anti-patterns and bad practices
- Introduction to CDC pattern
- Adopting cloud technologies and cloud services

Modernization strategies and data integration are paramount to thrive in the modern business landscape. By embracing modernization, avoiding anti-patterns such as poor data integration, and harnessing the power of modern cloud services, organizations can unlock the true potential of their data, drive innovation, and stay ahead of the competition. The journey toward modernization requires careful planning, a deep understanding of the organization's goals, and a commitment to leveraging cutting-edge technologies. With the right approach, businesses can navigate the complexities of modernization and pave the way for a successful digital transformation.

Application modernization strategies

Application modernization strategies involve updating and transforming existing legacy applications to meet the demands of the modern digital landscape. Legacy systems, often characterized by outdated technologies and rigid workflows, can impede an organization's ability to innovate, respond quickly to market demands, and leverage the full potential of emerging technologies. By implementing application modernization strategies, businesses can revitalize their software assets, enhance scalability, improve performance, and increase agility

Premature optimization is always dangerous; the belief that *monolithic* is synonymous with *legacy* is a mistake. As software engineers, we need to understand what the business needs and the context. Remember that no silver bullet in any solution includes monolithic and microservices architectural styles.

There are several approaches to application modernization, each with its benefits and considerations. Let's explore some of the common strategies and how to apply them effectively:

- Rehosting, or lift-and-shift, involves moving existing applications to a modern infrastructure without making significant code changes. This strategy offers faster migration with minimal disruption. Replatforming goes further by leveraging cloud-native features or services, such as scalability and managed databases, to optimize the application's performance. The key is to ensure compatibility and configuration adjustments when moving to new infrastructure—for example, cloud platforms such as **Amazon Web Services** (**AWS**), Microsoft Azure, and **Google Cloud Platform** (**GCP**).

- Refactoring focuses on improving the existing application's code base, structure, and architecture. This strategy involves making significant code changes, optimizing performance, enhancing scalability, and adopting modular or microservices architectures. The goal is to align the application with modern development practices, such as adopting containerization, decoupling components, and leveraging new frameworks or libraries.

- Rebuilding, also known as rewriting, involves starting from scratch while retaining the original application's functionality and business logic. This strategy allows leveraging modern development frameworks, tools, and architecture patterns. However, it requires careful planning, which can be time-consuming and resource-intensive. It is crucial to analyze the existing application's strengths and weaknesses to ensure that the new application meets business requirements effectively.

- The replacement strategy involves replacing the legacy application entirely with an off-the-shelf commercial software package or a **Software-as-a-Service** (**SaaS**) solution. This approach is suitable when the existing application no longer meets business needs, and it is more cost-effective to adopt a pre-built solution rather than invest in modernizing the legacy system.

Implementing legacy modernization strategies is essential when specific organizational triggers or challenges arise. Let's check common reasons to consider modernization, as legacy technology stacks:

- Often run on outdated technologies that are no longer supported or lack compatibility with modern software components. This can lead to security vulnerabilities, increased maintenance costs, and limited integration capabilities. Modernization helps mitigate these risks and ensures the application remains viable and secure.

- May need help to handle increasing workloads and deliver optimal performance. Modernization enables the application to scale horizontally or vertically, leverage cloud-based resources, and adopt modern architectural patterns, resulting in improved performance and scalability.

- Often hinder the adoption of agile development methodologies and DevOps practices due to their monolithic nature and rigid workflows. Application modernization promotes modular design, microservices, and containerization, enabling organizations to embrace agile methods, iterate quickly, and deploy changes more frequently.

- May fail to provide a modern user experience or keep up with industry standards, where user expectations evolve and the competition innovate constantly. Modernization strategies can enhance the application's user interface, introduce new features, and leverage emerging technologies such as **artificial intelligence** (**AI**), **machine learning** (**ML**), or mobile platforms.

Application modernization strategies are essential for organizations hoping to adapt, innovate, and remain competitive in the digital age. Choosing the appropriate modernization can minimize impacting your business/organization. But before starting this modernization process, review the requirements and goals to understand if it is necessary. Especially when we talk about the persistent layer, refactoring might be a risk and a considerable cost; it is more trivial than doing code refactoring with an **integrated development environment** (**IDE**). So, let's talk about those anti-patterns in data.

Avoiding data storage-related anti-patterns and bad practices

Several common anti-patterns and bad practices can hinder performance, scalability, and maintainability in an application's persistence layer. Understanding the difference between anti-patterns and harmful practices is crucial to accurately identify and mitigate these issues.

Anti-patterns are commonly observed in software development and can result from poor design decisions, a lack of understanding, or adherence to outdated practices. Anti-patterns in the persistence layer can include the following:

- **Object-relational impedance mismatch**: This anti-pattern occurs when there is a significant disconnect between the **object-oriented** (**OO**) model used in the application's code and the relational model used in the database. It can lead to excessive mapping and conversion logic, performance degradation, and complexity in maintaining data consistency. To avoid this anti-pattern, consider using **object-relational mapping** (**ORM**) frameworks that provide seamless integration between the application code and the database, reducing the impedance mismatch.

- **Data access in the presentation layer**: This anti-pattern involves performing data access operations directly in the presentation layer, such as in user interface components. It violates the principle of **separation of concerns** (**SoC**), leading to tightly coupled code, difficulty in maintaining and testing, and decreased reusability. While rarely recommended, there are a few good uses of data retrieval directly from the presentation layer. To address this, follow a layered architecture pattern (such as **Model View Controller** (**MVC**) or **Model-View-ViewModel** (**MVVM**), where data access operations are performed in a separate data access layer.

- **Querying the database in a loop**: This anti-pattern occurs when an application performs individual database queries within a loop instead of using bulk operations. It results in excessive database round trips, increased network overhead, and poor performance. To avoid this, optimize queries using batch processing, bulk inserts or updates, and caching mechanisms to minimize the number of database interactions.

Bad practices, on the other hand, refer to actions or habits that are generally recognized as inefficient, suboptimal, or detrimental to the overall quality of the software. Unlike anti-patterns, bad practices may not necessarily be recurring solutions but specific actions or choices that should be avoided. Some examples of bad practices in the persistence layer include the following:

- **Lack of connection pooling**: Failing to utilize connection pooling can lead to performance issues, especially in high-traffic applications. Opening and closing database connections for every request or operation can result in resource contention, increased overhead, and decreased scalability. Implementing connection pooling techniques provided by database drivers or frameworks to manage connections efficiently is essential.

- **Failure to use prepared statements or parameterized queries**: Constructing SQL queries by directly concatenating user input or dynamic values can expose the application to SQL injection attacks. It is essential to use prepared statements or parameterized queries, which ensure that user input is treated as data rather than executable code, thereby mitigating security risks.

To avoid anti-patterns and bad practices in the persistence layer, consider the following approaches:

- **Educate and train developers**: Ensure developers have a solid understanding of best practices, design patterns, and modern approaches to persistence. Provide training sessions, workshops, or resources to update them on industry standards and emerging technologies.

- **Follow design principles and patterns**: Apply design principles such as **SOLID** (which stands for **Single Responsibility, Open-Closed, Liskov Substitution, Interface Segregation, Dependency Inversion**) and use appropriate design patterns such as **Data Access Object** (**DAO**), repository, or ORM patterns. These principles and patterns promote SoC, modularity, and maintainability.

- **Use ORM or query builders**: Adopt ORM frameworks or query builders that provide abstraction layers to handle database interactions. ORM tools, such as Hibernate, **Entity Framework** (**EF**), or Sequelize, can help reduce object-relational impedance mismatches and handle data access operations efficiently.

- **Implement connection pooling**: Utilize connection pooling techniques provided by database drivers or frameworks to efficiently manage and reuse database connections. Connection pooling helps avoid the overhead of establishing new connections for each request, improving performance and scalability.

- **Sanitize user input and use prepared statements**: Always filter and sanitize user input and avoid directly concatenating dynamic values into SQL queries. Instead, utilize prepared statements or parameterized queries provided by the database APIs. This approach prevents SQL injection attacks and many user input errors by treating user input as a vulnerability rather than trustworthy input.

- **Perform code reviews and refactoring**: Conduct regular code reviews to identify anti-patterns, bad practices, and areas for improvement. Encourage a culture of continuous improvement where developers can provide feedback, suggest enhancements, and refactor code to align with best practices.

- **Test and benchmark performance**: Implement thorough unit tests and integration tests to validate the correctness of data access operations. Conduct performance testing and benchmarking to identify bottlenecks and optimize query execution times. Tools such as JMeter or Gatling can help simulate load and measure performance metrics.

- **Stay updated and engage in the community**: Stay informed about the latest advancements, updates, and best practices in persistence technologies and frameworks. Engage with the development community through forums, conferences, or online communities to share experiences, learn from others, and discover new techniques.

Adopting these practices and maintaining a proactive approach to code quality and performance optimization can significantly reduce the occurrence of anti-patterns and bad practices in the persistence layer, leading to more robust, maintainable, and scalable applications. Talking about good practices, in the following session, we'll explore the most modern one, CDC, and how it can help you on your journey on the persistence layer.

Introduction to CDC pattern

Change Data Capture (**CDC**) is a technique used to track and capture changes made to data in a database. It enables organizations to identify, capture, and propagate data changes in near-real time, providing a reliable and efficient data integration and synchronization method across different systems.

The following diagram shows a sample using the CDC pattern where we have a source that fires an event, and based on this event, each subscriber results in two database targets:

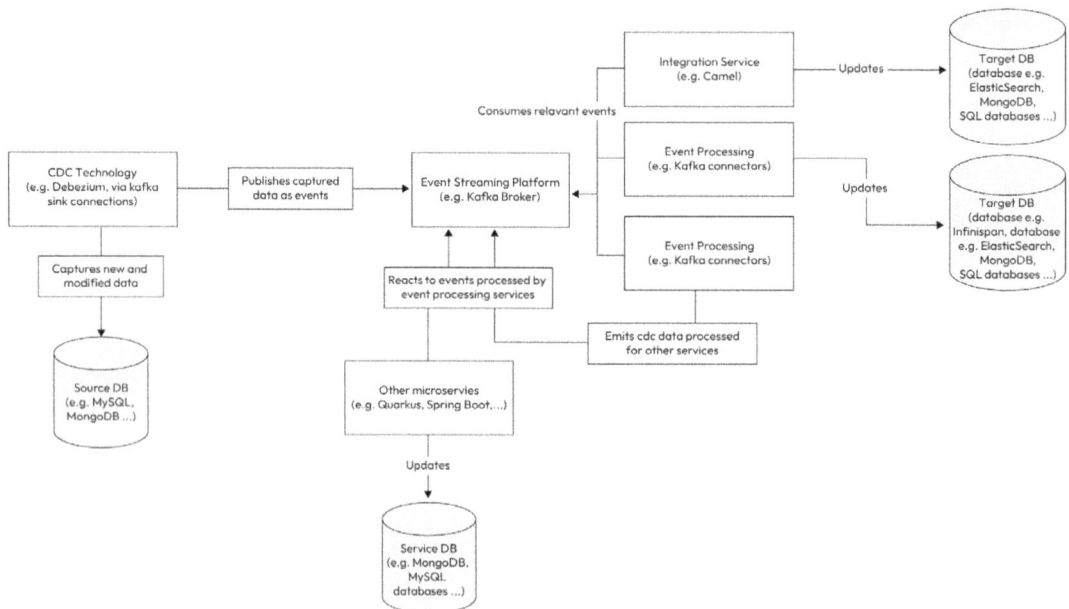

Figure 11.1 – CDC architecture representation

The process of CDC involves monitoring and capturing changes that occur at the database level, such as inserts, updates, and deletes, and emitting these as individual events. Instead of constantly polling the entire database for changes, CDC mechanisms track and capture only the modified data, reducing unnecessary overhead and improving performance.

Let's look at some further advantages of CDC:

- **Real-time data integration**: CDC enables organizations to capture and propagate data changes in near-real time, ensuring that the integrated systems can access the most up-to-date information. This real-time data integration allows more accurate reporting, analytics, and decision-making.

- **Improved data consistency**: By capturing and synchronizing data changes across different systems, CDC helps maintain data consistency and integrity. Updates made in one design can be automatically reflected in other systems, eliminating the need for manual data entry or batch processes.

- **Reduced latency**: CDC significantly reduces the latency between data changes and their availability in other systems. It is particularly important for scenarios where timely access to the latest data is critical, such as in financial transactions, inventory management, or real-time analytics.

- **Minimized impact on source systems**: Unlike traditional batch-based data integration approaches, CDC reduces the impact on the source systems by capturing changes incrementally rather than extracting and loading large datasets. It reduces the load on the source systems and avoids performance degradation.

- **Efficient data replication**: CDC enables efficient data replication across databases or systems. It only captures and transmits the changed data, reducing network bandwidth requirements and improving replication performance.

CDC is advantageous in the following scenarios:

- **Data warehousing and business intelligence (BI)**: CDC facilitates the integration of operational databases with data warehouses or data lakes, ensuring that analytics, transaction processing, and reporting systems have access to the most current data. It enables organizations to make data-driven decisions based on up-to-date information.

- **Microservices and event-driven architecture (EDA)**: CDC is valuable in EDA, where changes in one microservice trigger actions in other microservices. By capturing data changes in real time, CDC allows microservices to react to and process the latest data updates, ensuring consistency across the system.

- **Data synchronization and replication**: When multiple databases or systems need to be synchronized and kept up to date with each other, CDC provides an efficient mechanism for capturing and propagating changes. This is particularly relevant in scenarios involving distributed systems, multi-site deployments, or data replication for **disaster recovery (DR)** purposes.

- **Legacy system integration:** CDC can be used to integrate legacy systems with modern applications or databases. By capturing changes from legacy systems and propagating them to modern systems, organizations can leverage the capabilities of new technologies while maintaining the functionality of existing systems.

While CDC can be highly beneficial in many scenarios, there are certain situations where it may not be the most suitable approach. Here are some cases when CDC might not be the best choice:

- **Infrequent or low-impact data changes:** If the data changes in your system are irregular or have a minimal impact on downstream systems, implementing CDC might introduce unnecessary complexity. In such cases, traditional batch-based data extraction and loading processes may suffice.

- **Small-scale or simple applications:** For small-scale applications with limited data sources and straightforward integration requirements, the overhead of implementing CDC may outweigh the benefits. CDC is advantageous in complex, large-scale environments with multiple systems and databases.

- **Strict real-time requirements:** Although CDC provides near-real-time data integration, it might not be suitable for scenarios that demand immediate or sub-second data propagation. Alternative approaches such as event sourcing or streaming platforms may be more appropriate.

- **High-frequency and high-volume data changes:** If your system experiences an extremely high frequency or volume of data changes, implementing CDC may burden the source database and infrastructure. In such cases, it may be more efficient to consider alternative data integration techniques that can handle the scale effectively.

- **Data security and compliance concerns:** CDC may not be recommended when data security or compliance regulations strictly prohibit or limit data replication or movement. Evaluating and adhering to data governance and compliance requirements is crucial before implementing CDC.

- **Cost and resource constraints:** CDC implementations often require additional infrastructure, monitoring, and maintenance overhead. If you have budget constraints or limited resources to manage and support CDC, alternative data integration methods might be more feasible.

- **Legacy systems with limited capabilities:** Some legacy systems may need more functionality or capabilities to support CDC. In such cases, retrofitting CDC mechanisms into these systems may be challenging or impractical. Consider alternative integration approaches or explore options for modernizing the legacy system.

- **Lack of integration requirements:** CDC may not be necessary if your system does not require integration with other systems or databases and operates as a standalone application without data synchronization. Evaluate the integration needs and assess whether CDC adds value to your use case.

Remember—whether or not to use CDC depends on your system's requirements, complexity, and characteristics. It is essential to analyze your use case thoroughly, consider consider its up and downsides, and evaluate alternative data integration techniques before implementing CDC.

In summary, CDC is a powerful technique for capturing and propagating data changes in near-real time. Its benefits include the following:

- Real-time data integration

- Improved data consistency

- Reduced latency

- Minimized impact on source systems

- Efficient data replication

CDC is particularly valuable in data warehousing, microservices, EDA, data synchronization, replication, and legacy system integration

It is colossal work, and the good news is we can do it with others; public cloud offerings have multiplied and can help us a lot, especially in focusing more on the business and delegating what is not our core. When we talk about services in the cloud, one is implicit: DBaaS, where we don't need to be an expert or have one close to us; let's explore more about it in the next section.

Adopting cloud technologies and cloud services

Cloud services offer numerous advantages for the persistence layer of an application, providing enhanced database experiences and relieving organizations from various management and maintenance tasks. One particular service in this context is **Database-as-a-Service (DBaaS)**, which allows users to leverage the power of databases without the need for extensive expertise or infrastructure management.

DBaaS are traditional; setting up and managing databases involves significant effort, including hardware provisioning, software installation, configuration, and ongoing maintenance. However, DBaaS shifts these responsibilities to the **cloud service provider (CSP)**, enabling users to focus more on their application development and business logic.

Here are some ways in which cloud services, particularly DBaaS, can benefit the persistence layer:

- **Simplified database management**: DBaaS abstracts the complexities of managing databases, making it easier for developers and teams to handle the persistence layer. **Service providers (SPs)** handle tasks such as database installation, patching, and upgrades, relieving users of these time-consuming and sometimes error-prone activities.

- **Scalability and performance**: Cloud services offer the ability to scale databases vertically (increasing the resources of a single instance) or horizontally (adding more models to distribute the load). This scalability ensures that databases can handle increasing workloads and provide optimal performance to meet the application's demands.

- **Automated backup and recovery**: CSPs typically offer automatic database backup and recovery mechanisms. This ensures that regular backups are taken, reducing the risk of data loss. Additionally, in the event of a disaster or failure, the cloud provider can facilitate quick and efficient recovery, minimizing downtime and ensuring data availability.

- **High Availability (HA) and Fault Tolerance (FT)**: Cloud services often provide built-in mechanisms for achieving HA and FT in database systems. These include automatic failover, replication, and geographically distributed data centers. Such capabilities help ensure that the database remains accessible and resilient, even in the face of hardware failures or network outages.

- **Security and compliance**: CSPs prioritize safety and invest in robust infrastructure and data protection measures. They implement industry-standard security practices, encryption mechanisms, and compliance certifications. This allows organizations to benefit from the provider's expertise and focus on ensuring the security and compliance of their data without having to build and maintain such measures themselves.

- **Cost-efficiency**: Using cloud services for the persistence layer can be cost-effective, eliminating the need to invest in expensive hardware infrastructure and reducing ongoing maintenance and operational costs. Cloud providers typically offer pricing models that align with actual usage, allowing organizations to pay for the resources they consume rather than making significant upfront investments.

By leveraging cloud services, organizations can offload the responsibility of managing databases and focus on their core business objectives. The "somebody else's computer" joke highlights the advantage of delegating database-related issues to cloud providers. The SP takes care of tasks such as upgrading the database, backup and recovery, partitioning data, ensuring scalability, freeing up resources, and reducing the complexity of managing these aspects in-house.

Cloud services, particularly DBaaS, empower organizations to leverage robust, scalable, and highly available databases without needing extensive expertise or infrastructure management. With simplified management, enhanced scalability, automated backup and recovery, HA, security measures, and cost-efficiency, cloud services offer a valuable solution for the persistence layer of modern applications.

Summary

In this book, we explored various aspects of application modernization, focusing on strategies, anti-patterns, and ways to leverage modern cloud services to enhance the persistence layer of applications. We stressed the importance of adopting modernization strategies to keep pace with evolving technologies and meet the ever-changing needs of users and businesses.

We discussed the significance of avoiding anti-patterns and bad practices in the persistence layer, as they can hinder application performance, maintainability, and scalability. Developers can ensure a robust and efficient persistence layer by understanding these anti-patterns and their impact and by implementing best practices such as proper design principles, ORM frameworks, and connection pooling.

We also explored the CDC concept and its benefits in capturing and propagating data changes across systems. CDC enables real-time data integration, improved data consistency, and efficient data replication, making it a valuable technique in various scenarios such as data warehousing, microservices architectures, and data synchronization.

Furthermore, we delved into the advantages of cloud services, specifically DBaaS, in simplifying database management, enhancing scalability, providing automated backup and recovery, ensuring HA and FT, and addressing security and compliance concerns. By leveraging DBaaS, organizations can offload database-related tasks to cloud providers and focus on their core objectives.

As we conclude this book, we have covered fundamental concepts and practices related to application modernization, persistence layer optimization, and leveraging cloud services. The following chapters summarize our discussion, providing key takeaways and final considerations to guide your application modernization journey.

Remember—staying up to date with emerging technologies, adhering to best practices, and embracing cloud services can empower you to build modern, efficient, and scalable applications that meet the demands of today's dynamic digital landscape. By adopting a proactive approach to modernization and leveraging the power of cloud services, you can position your applications for success in the ever-evolving world of technology.

12
Final Considerations

We have explored the architectural perspective of persistence, delved into Jakarta EE and MicroProfile, examined modern persistence technologies and their trade-offs, and discussed the essential aspects of persistence in the cloud era. This final chapter will reflect on the key insights and considerations gathered throughout our persistence journey. Now, let us combine the lessons learned and draw some conclusions:

- **Embracing the architectural perspective**: Understanding the architectural perspective is crucial for designing robust and scalable persistence solutions. A holistic approach that aligns persistence with the overall system architecture ensures we can effectively manage complexity and evolve our applications over time. By considering factors such as data modeling, transaction management, caching, and scalability, we can build systems that meet the demands of modern applications.

- **Jakarta EE and MicroProfile**: The Jakarta EE and MicroProfile specifications provide a standardized foundation for building enterprise Java applications. These frameworks offer many persistence-related APIs and features that simplify development. By adhering to these standards, we can benefit from portability, interoperability, and a vibrant ecosystem of compatible libraries and tools.

- **Modern persistence technologies and trade-offs**: The landscape of persistence technologies has evolved significantly, offering developers diverse options. We explored the trade-offs associated with different approaches, such as relational databases, NoSQL databases, and object-relational mapping frameworks. Each technology has its strengths and weaknesses, and the choice depends on specific project requirements. Understanding the trade-offs helps us make informed decisions and optimize the persistence layer for our applications.

- **Persistence essentials in the cloud era**: The rise of cloud computing has introduced new challenges and opportunities in the persistence domain. Cloud-native persistence solutions such as managed database services, distributed caching, and event-driven architectures enable us to build resilient, elastic, and cost-efficient applications. We discussed essential considerations for achieving persistence in the cloud, including scalability, data consistency, multi-region deployments, and serverless architectures.

- **The importance of continuous learning**: Persistence is dynamic, with new technologies and approaches emerging regularly. As developers, it is essential to cultivate a mindset of continuous learning and stay updated with the latest trends. It includes monitoring advancements in Jakarta EE and MicroProfile, exploring new database technologies, and understanding best practices for cloud-native persistence. By embracing a learning mindset, we can adapt to evolving requirements and leverage the full potential of persistence in our applications.

In this chapter, we'll explore these topics further:

- The power of tests and leading with data-domain tests

- Don't underestimate the documentation; this helps scalability

- The software architecture is there, with or without architects

The power of tests - How to lead with data-domain tests

Ensuring data and behavior consistency is a critical aspect of building robust and reliable applications. Application bugs can introduce inconsistencies in data, leading to unexpected behavior and incorrect results. Implementing effective testing strategies can help identify and prevent such issues. Integration testing and data-driven testing are effective approaches to verifying the correctness and consistency of the application's behavior.

Integration testing involves testing the interactions between different components of an application to ensure they work together as expected. It is particularly relevant when trying the persistence layer, as it allows you to validate the integration between the application and the underlying data storage systems.

Data-driven testing validates the application's behavior with different input datasets. By systematically varying the input data and comparing the expected results with the actual outputs, you can identify inconsistencies and detect any potential bugs that might impact data consistency.

Java has several testing frameworks and tools to facilitate integration and data-driven testing. JUnit Jupiter is a popular testing framework that provides a robust and flexible platform for writing and executing tests. It offers various annotations, assertions, and test execution life cycle callbacks to support integration testing scenarios.

AssertJ is another powerful library that enhances the readability and expressiveness of assertions in tests. It provides a fluent API for performing claims on various data types, making validating expected results easier and ensuring data consistency.

Test Container is a Java library that simplifies the testing of applications that depend on external resources such as databases, message brokers, or other containers. It allows you to define and manage lightweight, isolated containers for your integration tests, providing a convenient way to ensure consistent behavior when working with external systems.

Remember, testing is a crucial part of the development process, and investing in solid testing practices will help you identify and resolve data consistency issues early, leading to more robust and trustworthy applications. After tests, let's move on to an underestimated topic in software development: documentation. It reduces the number of meetings, breaks down the silos, and can help you with distributed systems.

Do not underestimate the importance of documentation

Documentation is crucial in software development, enabling teams to achieve scalability, streamline onboarding processes, break down knowledge silos, and ensure everyone is aligned and moving in the right direction.

As projects and teams grow, the need for scalability becomes evident. Documentation is a knowledge repository allowing teams to effectively share information and best practices. Developers can easily understand the system's structure and collaborate efficiently by documenting architectural decisions, design patterns, and coding conventions. This scalability ensures that as teams expand or new members join, the collective knowledge is preserved, and onboarding becomes smoother.

Onboarding new team members can be a time-consuming and challenging process. Documentation provides a resource for new developers to quickly familiarize themselves with the project's architecture, design principles, and coding standards. It flattens the learning curve and enables newcomers to learn quickly. Well-documented systems also facilitate knowledge transfer during employee transitions, minimizing the impact of personnel changes on project continuity.

In many organizations, knowledge silos can hinder collaboration and productivity and tend to cause errors. When knowledge resides with specific individuals, it becomes difficult for others to access and benefit from it. Documentation helps break down these silos by capturing and sharing expertise across the team. By documenting architectural decisions, integration patterns, and implementation details, teams can democratize knowledge and empower everyone to contribute to the project's success.

Documentation serves as a compass, guiding the team in the right direction. It captures the "why" behind architectural choices, design decisions, and coding practices. By documenting these rationales, teams establish a shared understanding and vision for the project. It ensures everyone is aligned with the system's purpose, goals, and desired outcomes. Documentation is a reference point, allowing developers to make informed decisions and avoid diverging paths.

Documentation plays a crucial role in the context of distributed systems by providing clarity and understanding of the system's architecture, integration points, and communication protocols. It acts as a means to communicate the system's structure, behavior, and dependencies to all stakeholders, ensuring a common language and understanding.

The documentation defines integration points, data formats, and communication protocols, facilitating seamless interoperability. It captures fault tolerance, resilience, and scalability strategies, enabling teams to design and implement systems that gracefully handle failures and optimize performance. Detailed documentation outlines deployment architectures, configuration parameters, and troubleshooting steps, aiding in the smooth setup, management, and maintenance of distributed systems. Overall, documentation in distributed systems enhances understanding, collaboration, and effective leadership, leading to improved reliability, performance, and system quality.

The C4 model, popularized by Simon Brown, provides a robust framework for documenting software architecture. It employs a hierarchical structure that allows teams to zoom in and out, giving high-level overviews and detailed views of the system's components and their interactions. The C4 model acts as a "Google Maps" for architecture, enabling teams to communicate and visualize complex systems effectively.

In addition to architectural documentation, it is crucial to focus on tactical documentation at the code level. Clear and concise code comments, descriptive functions, and variable names enhance code readability and maintainability. It includes well-documented code, informative README files, and comprehensive changelogs. README files provide an overview of the project, installation instructions, and usage examples, facilitating collaboration with other developers. changelogs keep track of the version history, documenting feature additions, bug fixes, and other notable changes.

Documentation is a powerful tool in software development, aiding team scalability, facilitating onboarding, breaking down knowledge silos, and ensuring alignment and direction from documenting architectural decisions to providing tactical documentation at the code level, investing time and effort in creating comprehensive and accessible documentation.

If, after discussing documentation and testing, you are still here, let's finish this chapter with a topic that we also don't enjoy, or at least has become a red flag because of bad practices we've encountered in the past: architecture.

Architecture without architects

In the past, companies often associated software architecture with a centralized area of command and control, which may not have resulted in a better experience for engineers. However, it is crucial to recognize that software architecture goes beyond having a sector or team setup. It plays a significant role in the entire organization's success.

Software architecture encompasses a system's fundamental structure and design, encompassing its components, interactions, and overall organization. It is the blueprint for building robust, scalable, and maintainable systems. While some people perceive architecture as an optional concern, architecture is always present, whether we notice it or not.

A well-designed software architecture provides numerous benefits, especially in distributed systems. Good architecture comes in handy, especially when taking into consideration that distributed systems:

- Often need to handle increased loads and accommodate growing user bases. A well-thought-out architecture considers scalability, enabling the system to handle higher traffic volumes and adapt to changing demands. It allows for horizontal scaling by distributing components across multiple nodes and leveraging load-balancing techniques, resulting in better performance and responsiveness.

- Are prone to failures and network disruptions. With a robust architecture, you can incorporate fault tolerance and resilience strategies. It includes redundancy, replication, error-handling mechanisms, and the ability to recover gracefully from failures. By designing for resilience, your system can maintain availability and continue functioning despite individual component failures.

- Often involve multiple components and services that must work together seamlessly. A well-designed architecture promotes modularity, encapsulation, and loose coupling between components. This modular approach allows for the more accessible development, testing, deployment, and evolution of individual members, enabling flexibility and adaptability to changing business requirements.

- Frequently interact with external services, APIs, and data sources. A well-defined architecture facilitates seamless integration and interoperability with these external systems. By clearly defining communication protocols, API contracts, and integration patterns, the architecture enables smooth interactions, making it easier to consume or expose services and exchange data with external entities.

- Must be designed to handle the demands of large-scale data processing and communication. A well-architected system can optimize performance by considering data locality, caching strategies, load balancing, and efficient communication protocols. You can minimize latency, bandwidth usage, and resource contention through careful architectural choices, ultimately improving the system's overall performance.

In conclusion, software architecture is not merely a sector or team but a crucial aspect of the entire organization's success. Good architecture helps build scalable, resilient, flexible, and performant distributed systems. By considering factors such as scalability, resilience, flexibility, interoperability, and performance optimization, a well-designed architecture sets the foundation for building distributed systems that meet the challenges and complexities of modern software development.

Summary

To wrap it up, we express our sincere gratitude to you, the reader, for accompanying us to the end of this book. We hope the knowledge and insights shared throughout these pages are as valuable to you, as it were to us. Use this book whenever needed, as a helpful resource to understanding the intricacies of persistence in software development. Have in mind that this book is just the beginning of your persistence journey as a software engineer. The persistence field is continually evolving, with new technologies, patterns, and trade-offs emerging. Embrace this opportunity to learn and grow, staying curious and open-minded to recent advancements in persistence. By applying the principles and concepts covered in this book and remaining eager to explore further, you will be well equipped to tackle the challenges and opportunities in your journey as a software engineer. Again, thank you, and we wish you great success in your persistent endeavors.

Further reading

- *Effective Software Testing: A Developer's Guide* by *Maurizio Aniche*, to delve deeper into effective software testing practices. This book provides valuable insights and techniques for improving your testing skills, including strategies for integration testing, data-driven testing, and other essential testing concepts. By leveraging the knowledge shared in this book, you can enhance the quality and reliability of your software through comprehensive and effective testing.

- *Fundamentals of Software Architecture an Engineering Approach* by *Neal Ford* is a highly recommended book that provides valuable insights into software architecture principles, patterns, and best practices. It covers essential topics such as architectural styles, design principles, scalability, modularity, and so on. By studying this book, you can enhance your understanding of software architecture and apply it effectively to distributed systems.

- *Docs for Developers: An Engineer's Field Guide to Technical Writing* by *Jared Bhatti, Sarah Corleissen, Jen Lambourne*, and *David Nunez* is a comprehensive and practical book that is an invaluable resource for developers looking to enhance their technical writing skills. Written by experts in the field, this book delves into the nuances of practical documentation, offering insights, strategies, and best practices tailored specifically to the needs of developers.

- *The C4 Model for Visualising Software Architecture* by *Simon Brown* is a transformative book that offers developers a comprehensive framework for effectively visualizing and communicating software architecture. Authored by experienced practitioners, this book introduces the C4 model – a pragmatic approach that simplifies complex architectural designs into a series of hierarchical diagrams. By providing a clear and consistent language for representing software systems, components, containers, and code, the C4 model facilitates effective communication and collaboration among developers, architects, and stakeholders.

Index

‹packt›

www.packtpub.com

Subscribe to our online digital library for full access to over 7,000 books and videos, as well as industry leading tools to help you plan your personal development and advance your career. For more information, please visit our website.

Why subscribe?

- Spend less time learning and more time coding with practical eBooks and Videos from over 4,000 industry professionals

- Improve your learning with Skill Plans built especially for you

- Get a free eBook or video every month

- Fully searchable for easy access to vital information

- Copy and paste, print, and bookmark content

Did you know that Packt offers eBook versions of every book published, with PDF and ePub files available? You can upgrade to the eBook version at packtpub.com and as a print book customer, you are entitled to a discount on the eBook copy. Get in touch with us at customercare@packtpub.com for more details.

At www.packtpub.com, you can also read a collection of free technical articles, sign up for a range of free newsletters, and receive exclusive discounts and offers on Packt books and eBooks.

Other Books You May Enjoy

If you enjoyed this book, you may be interested in these other books by Packt:

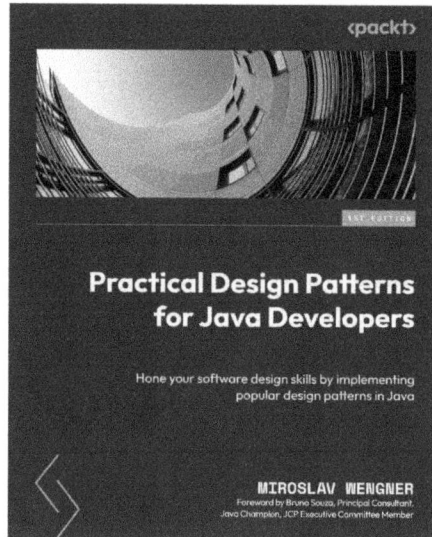

Practical Design Patterns for Java Developers

Miroslav Wengner

ISBN: 978-1-80461-467-9

- Understand the most common problems that can be solved using Java design patterns
- Uncover Java building elements, their usages, and concurrency possibilities
- Optimize a vehicle memory footprint with the Flyweight Pattern
- Explore one-to-many relations between instances with the observer pattern
- Discover how to route vehicle messages by using the visitor pattern
- Utilize and control vehicle resources with the thread-pool pattern
- Understand the penalties caused by anti-patterns in software design

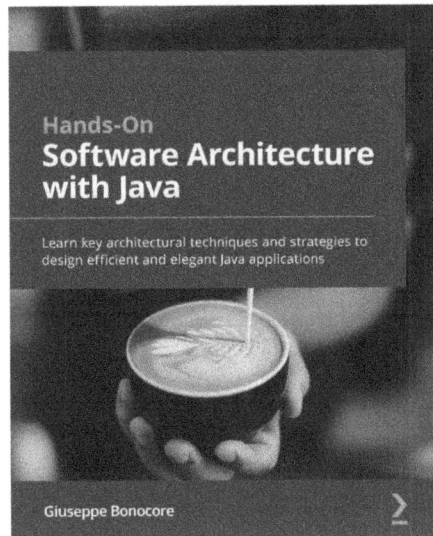

Hands-On Software Architecture with Java

Giuseppe Bonocore

ISBN: 978-1-80020-730-1

- Understand the importance of requirements engineering, including functional versus non-functional requirements
- Explore design techniques such as domain-driven design, test-driven development (TDD), and behavior-driven development
- Discover the mantras of selecting the right architectural patterns for modern applications
- Explore different integration patterns
- Enhance existing applications with essential cloud-native patterns and recommended practices
- Address cross-cutting considerations in enterprise applications regardless of architectural choices and application type

Packt is searching for authors like you

If you're interested in becoming an author for Packt, please visit `authors.packtpub.com` and apply today. We have worked with thousands of developers and tech professionals, just like you, to help them share their insight with the global tech community. You can make a general application, apply for a specific hot topic that we are recruiting an author for, or submit your own idea.

Share Your Thoughts

Now you've finished *Persistence Best Practices for Java Applications*, we'd love to hear your thoughts! If you purchased the book from Amazon, please click here to go straight to the Amazon review page for this book and share your feedback or leave a review on the site that you purchased it from.

Your review is important to us and the tech community and will help us make sure we're delivering excellent quality content.

Download a free PDF copy of this book

Thanks for purchasing this book!

Do you like to read on the go but are unable to carry your print books everywhere?

Is your eBook purchase not compatible with the device of your choice?

Don't worry, now with every Packt book you get a DRM-free PDF version of that book at no cost.

Read anywhere, any place, on any device. Search, copy, and paste code from your favorite technical books directly into your application.

The perks don't stop there, you can get exclusive access to discounts, newsletters, and great free content in your inbox daily

Follow these simple steps to get the benefits:

1. Scan the QR code or visit the link below

https://packt.link/free-ebook/9781837631278

2. Submit your proof of purchase
3. That's it! We'll send your free PDF and other benefits to your email directly

Milton Keynes UK
Ingram Content Group UK Ltd.
UKHW031828131123
432508UK00007B/77

9 781837 631278